EXAMINING BIODIVERSITY HOTSPOT

HOTSPOT

NATURE'S DISTINCTIVENESS SCAN

TOM FERRY J

COPYRIGHT © 2023 BY TOM FERRY J

DISCLAIMER

The information and content contained in this book, "Examining Biodiversity Hotspot: Nature's Distinctiveness Scan," are provided for general informational purposes only. The author and publisher make no representations or warranties of any kind, express or implied, about the completeness, accuracy, reliability, suitability, or availability of the information and content contained herein.

The author and publisher disclaim any liability for any loss or damage arising from the use of this book or its content. Readers are encouraged to seek professional advice and conduct their own research and due diligence when making decisions or drawing conclusions based on the information presented in this book.

While every effort has been made to ensure the accuracy and completeness of the information contained in this book, the author and publisher do not assume any responsibility for errors, omissions, or inaccuracies, or for any consequences arising from the use of the information or content provided herein.

The views and opinions expressed in this book are those of the author and do not necessarily reflect the official policy or position of any organization, institution, or individual mentioned or referenced within.

TABLE OF CONTENT

INTRODUCTION

Prepare to embark on an awe-inspiring journey into the heart of our planet's most remarkable and mysterious biodiversity hotspots. In "Examining Biodiversity Hotspot: Nature's Distinctiveness Scan," I invite you to join me in a captivating exploration of Earth's hidden gems—places were life flourishes in astonishing diversity and abundance.

As we dive into the pages of this book, we'll uncover the secrets of these ecological treasures, where every species, no matter how big or small, plays a crucial role in the intricate web of life. From the lush rainforests teeming with vibrant colors and melodies to the arid deserts where life adapts in extraordinary ways, each hotspot has a unique story to tell.

But this journey is not just about admiring the beauty of nature; it's about understanding the delicate balance that sustains life on our planet. We'll delve into the science behind these hotspots, exploring the mechanisms that drive evolution, conservation efforts, and the urgent need to protect these invaluable ecosystems.

Whether you're a seasoned environmental enthusiast or a curious newcomer to the wonders of biodiversity, this book is your key to unlocking the mysteries of our planet's natural wonders. It's a call to action, a celebration of diversity, and an invitation to become a steward of our Earth's incredible wealth of life.

So, without further ado, let's begin our adventure! Join me in the pages that follow as we unravel the intricacies of nature's distinctiveness and discover the breathtaking beauty that lies within biodiversity hotspots.

CHAPTER 1: INTRODUCTION

THE MARVELS OF BIODIVERSITY HOTSPOTS

Biodiversity hotspots are among the most astonishing and captivating natural wonders on our planet. These regions, which cover a mere fraction of the Earth's surface, harbor an extraordinary wealth of life, earning them the title of "hotspots." In this chapter, we embark on a journey to unravel the marvels of biodiversity hotspots—nature's hidden treasure troves of life.

What Defines a Biodiversity Hotspot?

A biodiversity hotspot is not just any ecologically rich area; it is a specific classification based on scientific criteria. To earn the designation of a hotspot, an area must meet two essential criteria:

High Species Richness: Hotspots must contain a high number of plant species that are both unique to the region (endemic) and threatened with extinction. This criterion is a testament to the exceptional diversity of life found within these areas.

Severe Habitat Loss: Hotspots are also characterized by significant habitat loss, typically due to human activities such as deforestation, urbanization, and agriculture. This unfortunate reality underscores the urgent need for conservation efforts to protect these vital regions.

The Global Distribution of Hotspots

While biodiversity hotspots exist all over the world, their distribution is not uniform. Currently, there are 36 recognized hotspots spread across six continents. Some of the most well-known hotspots include the Amazon Rainforest in South America, the Coral Triangle in Southeast Asia, and the Cape Floristic Region in South Africa.

Hotspot Highlights: An Ecological Kaleidoscope

Biodiversity hotspots are like ecological kaleidoscopes, each offering a unique blend of species and ecosystems. Here are just a few of the fascinating features found within these hotspots:

1. Rainforests: Many hotspots, such as the Amazon and Congo Basins, are home to lush rainforests teeming with life. The canopy of these rainforests is a vibrant world of color, sound, and undiscovered species.

2. Islands: Isolated islands, like the Galápagos and Madagascar, have given rise to extraordinary evolutionary adaptations. Unique species have evolved in isolation, making these islands living laboratories of evolution.

3. Coral Reefs: Hotspots often include marine ecosystems like coral reefs. These underwater wonderlands are biodiversity hotspots in their own right, hosting a stunning array of marine life.

4. Mountains: High-altitude hotspots, such as the Himalayas, showcase the remarkable adaptations of flora and fauna to extreme conditions. These mountains are cradles of biodiversity.

5. Unique Flora and Fauna: Hotspots feature plant and animal species found nowhere else on Earth. The intricacies of coevolution and ecological niches are on full display.

The Conservation Imperative

While biodiversity hotspots are awe-inspiring, they are also incredibly vulnerable. Habitat destruction, climate change, and overexploitation of resources threaten the very existence of the species that call these areas home. Conservation efforts are essential to safeguard the unique biodiversity found within hotspots.

In the chapters that follow, we will delve deeper into the individual hotspots across the globe. We will explore their distinctiveness, the challenges they face, and the conservation initiatives that are working tirelessly to protect these invaluable treasures. By understanding and appreciating the marvels of biodiversity hotspots, we take the first step towards becoming stewards of our planet's most exceptional ecosystems.

WHY BIODIVERSITY MATTERS

Biodiversity, short for biological diversity, is the variety of life on Earth—ranging from the tiniest microorganisms to the largest mammals and everything in between. It encompasses not only the sheer number of species but also their genetic diversity and the multitude of ecosystems they inhabit. Biodiversity is not just a scientific concept; it is a fundamental aspect of our planet's health and well-being. In this section, we explore why biodiversity matters profoundly to us and the planet we call home.

1. Ecosystem Stability and Resilience

Biodiversity is the bedrock of ecosystem stability and resilience. In diverse ecosystems, different species play unique roles, ensuring that if one species declines or disappears, others can step in to maintain vital functions. This diversity enhances the ecosystem's ability to withstand disturbances, adapt to changing conditions, and recover from disasters, such as wildfires, diseases, or extreme weather events.

2. Food Security and Agriculture

Biodiversity is essential for food production and agriculture. A variety of plant and animal species provide us with food, not only from traditional crops and livestock but also from wild species. Genetic diversity within crops is crucial for breeding resilient, disease-resistant, and high-yielding varieties that can feed a growing global population.

3. Medicines and Health

Many of the medicines and treatments we rely on come from nature. Biodiversity is a vast reservoir of potential pharmaceuticals, as many plant and animal species produce compounds with medicinal properties. Studying biodiversity can lead to breakthroughs in medicine, offering treatments for various diseases and health conditions.

4. Economic Benefits

Biodiversity provides significant economic benefits. Ecosystem services, such as pollination, water purification, and soil fertility, have an estimated global value of trillions of dollars annually. Healthy ecosystems contribute to industries like tourism, agriculture, and fisheries, supporting livelihoods and economic growth.

5. Cultural and Aesthetic Value

Biodiversity is deeply intertwined with human culture and spirituality. It plays a central role in indigenous knowledge systems, traditional practices, and rituals. Beyond its practical benefits, biodiversity enriches our lives through its beauty, inspiring art, literature, and a sense of wonder about the natural world.

6. Climate Regulation

Forests, wetlands, and oceans are among the planet's most effective carbon sinks. Biodiverse ecosystems absorb and store carbon dioxide, helping to mitigate climate change. Mangroves and coastal ecosystems also protect against storm surges and sea-level rise.

7. Ethical and Moral Considerations

Biodiversity has intrinsic value—it has a right to exist, whether or not it benefits humans directly. Many people believe that preserving biodiversity is a moral and ethical duty, recognizing the intrinsic worth of all living beings and the interconnectedness of life on Earth.

8. Resilience to Disease

Biodiversity can act as a buffer against disease outbreaks. In ecosystems with high biodiversity, disease pathogens are less likely to spread rapidly because there are more species to act as "dilution hosts," reducing the chances of a single pathogen infecting a large portion of the population.

9. Scientific Discovery

Biodiversity is a source of endless scientific discovery. New species, behaviors, and ecological relationships continue to be uncovered, expanding our understanding of the natural world and providing insights into the functioning of ecosystems.

Biodiversity is not just an abstract concept but a critical component of our daily lives and the functioning of the planet. It sustains us with food, medicine, and economic opportunities, enriches our cultures and aesthetics, and plays a pivotal role in maintaining a stable and habitable Earth. Recognizing the value of biodiversity is the first step in protecting it for future generations.

PURPOSE AND SCOPE OF THIS BOOK

In the pages that follow, we embark on a journey to explore the remarkable world of biodiversity hotspots, a topic of critical importance for the future of our planet. This chapter outlines the purpose and scope of this book, providing insight into what you can expect to discover within its covers.

1. Unveiling the Wonders of Biodiversity Hotspots

The primary purpose of this book is to unveil the wonders of biodiversity hotspots to readers of all backgrounds and interests. Whether you are a seasoned environmental enthusiast, a student eager to learn, or simply a curious explorer of the natural world, our goal is to take you on a captivating journey through these ecological treasure troves.

2. Understanding the Significance

We delve deep into the significance of biodiversity hotspots, exploring why they are so vital for the health of our planet. These hotspots are not just exotic locales; they are critical centers of biodiversity that play a profound role in shaping global ecosystems.

Through our exploration, you will gain a comprehensive understanding of why conserving these regions is imperative.

3. Highlighting Unique Features

Each chapter of this book focuses on a specific biodiversity hotspot or region, highlighting its unique features, exceptional species, and ecological marvels. From the lush rainforests of the Amazon to the high-altitude treasures of the Himalayas, we aim to paint a vivid picture of the diverse ecosystems and life forms found within these hotspots.

4. Conservation and Preservation

An essential aspect of our journey is exploring the challenges that biodiversity hotspots face, from habitat destruction to climate change. However, we don't stop at highlighting the problems. We also discuss the conservation efforts and strategies that are making a difference in preserving these invaluable regions for future generations.

5. Encouraging Stewardship

Beyond education and exploration, this book aims to inspire stewardship. We believe that by understanding the beauty and importance of biodiversity hotspots, readers can become advocates for conservation. We encourage you to engage with the information presented here and consider how you can contribute to the protection of these precious ecosystems.

6. A Global Perspective

Our exploration spans the globe, from the rainforests of South America to the islands of the Pacific. This book offers a comprehensive overview of biodiversity hotspots on multiple continents, providing a global perspective on these remarkable regions.

7. Accessibility and Engagement

We have designed this book to be accessible to a wide audience. While it delves into scientific concepts, it does so in a way that is approachable and engaging. It is our hope that readers of all backgrounds will find this book both informative and enjoyable.

In essence, the purpose of "Examining Biodiversity Hotspot: Nature's Distinctiveness Scan" is to shed light on the extraordinary world of biodiversity hotspots and inspire a sense of wonder, understanding, and responsibility for these critical ecosystems. As we embark on this journey together, let your curiosity guide you, and may you find inspiration to become a champion for the conservation of our planet's natural wonders.

CHAPTER 2: WHAT ARE BIODIVERSITY HOTSPOTS?

DEFINING BIODIVERSITY HOTSPOTS

Biodiversity hotspots are not just geographical regions; they are ecological treasures that have been carefully defined based on scientific criteria. In this section, we delve into what defines a biodiversity hotspot and how these criteria help identify and prioritize areas of exceptional biological importance.

The Origins of the Concept

The concept of biodiversity hotspots was first introduced by Dr. Norman Myers in a groundbreaking paper published in 1988. Myers proposed that certain regions on Earth held unique ecological significance due to their exceptionally high levels of biodiversity and high levels of threat from human activities. This idea has since become a crucial framework for conservation efforts worldwide.

Key Criteria for Hotspot Classification

To be classified as a biodiversity hotspot, a region must meet two primary criteria:

1. High Species Richness: Biodiversity hotspots are characterized by a remarkable concentration of species. Specifically, they must have a high number of plant species that are both endemic and threatened. Let's break down what these terms mean:

Endemic Species: These are species found nowhere else on Earth but within the defined hotspot boundaries. Endemic species are often highly specialized and adapted to the unique conditions of the hotspot.

Threatened Species: These are species that face a significant risk of extinction. Threats can include habitat destruction, pollution, over-exploitation, invasive species, and climate change.

2. Severe Habitat Loss: The second criterion is a sobering one—biodiversity hotspots must also suffer from severe habitat loss. This typically results from human activities such as deforestation, urbanization, agriculture, and infrastructure development. The presence of these threats underscores the urgent need for conservation efforts in these areas.

Why These Criteria Matter

The criteria for defining biodiversity hotspots are not arbitrary; they serve a crucial purpose in conservation science and practice:

1. Targeted Conservation: By identifying regions that meet these criteria, conservation efforts can be strategically directed to protect areas with the highest ecological value and the most urgent need for preservation.

2. Maximizing Impact: Biodiversity hotspots represent a relatively small portion of the Earth's surface, yet they contain a disproportionately large share of the world's biodiversity. Focusing on these areas allows conservationists to maximize their impact.

3. Raising Awareness: The concept of biodiversity hotspots has helped raise awareness about the global biodiversity crisis. It emphasizes the urgency of protecting these vital regions before irreplaceable species and ecosystems are lost forever.

4. Scientific Research: Biodiversity hotspots are rich subjects for scientific study. Researchers can explore the unique adaptations, ecological interactions, and evolutionary processes that occur within these regions, deepening our understanding of life on Earth.

Biodiversity hotspots are not merely geographical designations; they are regions that meet specific scientific criteria for exceptional biodiversity and severe threats. Recognizing and defining these hotspots is a pivotal step in the global effort to preserve our planet's biological diversity and the ecological services it provides.

CRITERIA FOR HOTSPOT CLASSIFICATION

Biodiversity hotspots are not arbitrary designations; they are carefully defined based on specific criteria that help identify regions of exceptional ecological importance. These criteria are fundamental in guiding conservation efforts and prioritizing areas for protection. In this section, we delve into the key criteria for hotspot classification.

1. High Species Richness

At the core of hotspot classification is the concept of high species richness. This criterion recognizes regions with an unusually large number of plant species. However, it's not just about quantity; it's also about the uniqueness of these species within the hotspot's boundaries.

Endemic Species: A significant portion of the plant species in a hotspot must be endemic, meaning they are found nowhere else on Earth but within the defined hotspot area. Endemic species are often highly specialized and uniquely adapted to the local environmental conditions.

Threatened Species: Another aspect of species' richness involves identifying species that face a significant risk of extinction. Threatened species can be categorized as vulnerable, endangered, or critically endangered based on the level of risk they face. The presence of threatened species within a hotspot signifies the urgent need for conservation efforts.

2. Severe Habitat Loss

The second major criterion for hotspot classification is the extent of habitat loss within the region. Habitat loss is typically caused by human activities, such as deforestation, urbanization, agriculture, mining, and infrastructure development. The severity of habitat loss in a hotspot is often measured as a percentage of the original habitat that has been converted or degraded.

Why These Criteria Matter

These criteria serve several crucial purposes in the context of biodiversity conservation:

1. Targeted Conservation Efforts: By identifying regions that meet these criteria, conservationists can strategically focus their efforts on areas with the highest ecological value and the most pressing need for protection.

2. Maximizing Conservation Impact: Biodiversity hotspots represent a relatively small portion of the Earth's surface but host a disproportionately large share of global biodiversity. Prioritizing these areas allows conservation efforts to have a maximum impact in terms of species and ecosystem preservation.

3. Raising Awareness: The concept of biodiversity hotspots helps raise awareness about the global biodiversity crisis. It underscores the urgency of protecting these vital regions before unique species and ecosystems are lost forever.

4. Scientific Study: Biodiversity hotspots are rich subjects for scientific research. They provide opportunities to study the unique adaptations, ecological interactions, and evolutionary processes that occur within these regions, contributing to our broader understanding of life on Earth.

Biodiversity hotspots are defined by specific criteria that emphasize both the richness and uniqueness of species within the region, as well as the severity of habitat loss due to human activities. Recognizing and applying these criteria are essential steps in the global effort to preserve Earth's biological diversity and maintain the ecological balance upon which all life depends.

GLOBAL DISTRIBUTION OF HOTSPOTS

Biodiversity hotspots are scattered like precious gems across the Earth's surface, each one shining with unique ecological significance. In this section, we explore the global distribution of these hotspots, highlighting their locations and the remarkable biodiversity they harbor.

From Tropical Rainforests to Arctic Tundra's

Biodiversity hotspots are not confined to a single type of ecosystem or climate zone. They can be found in various regions and continents, each with its distinct characteristics. Here are some examples of the global distribution of hotspots:

1. Tropical Rainforests: Some of the most famous hotspots are situated in tropical rainforests. The Amazon Rainforest in South America, the Congo Basin in Africa, and the Sundaland hotspot in Southeast Asia are renowned for their lush green canopies, teeming with an incredible array of plant and animal species.

2. Arid and Semi-Arid Regions: Hotspots also exist in arid and semi-arid regions, where life has adapted to challenging conditions. The Succulent Karoo in South Africa, the Mediterranean Basin, and the California Floristic Province in the United States are examples of hotspots in these drier climates.

3. Islands: Isolated islands have given rise to unique species and ecosystems due to their isolation. The Galápagos Islands in the Pacific Ocean, Madagascar in the Indian Ocean, and the Philippines in Southeast Asia are known for their exceptional biodiversity and endemism.

4. Mountains: High-altitude regions, including the Himalayas in Asia and the Andes in South America, are also home to biodiversity hotspots. These mountainous areas are centers of diversity for species adapted to extreme conditions.

5. Coastal and Marine Ecosystems: Biodiversity hotspots extend to coastal and marine environments. The Coral Triangle in Southeast Asia is a prime example, boasting the highest diversity of coral

species in the world, along with a multitude of marine life.

6. Temperate Forests: Even temperate regions can host biodiversity hotspots. The Mediterranean Basin and the Caucasus hotspot in Europe are characterized by their diverse flora and fauna, including numerous endemic species.

7. Islands in the Sky: Some hotspots are found in unique environments known as "sky islands." These are high-elevation mountain ranges surrounded by lower-altitude terrain. The Eastern Arc Mountains in Africa and the Madrean Pine-Oak Woodlands of North America are examples.

THE CONSERVATION CHALLENGE

While the global distribution of hotspots highlights the incredible biodiversity found across different ecosystems and regions, it also underscores the immense conservation challenge we face. Many of these hotspots are under severe threat from human activities, including deforestation, habitat destruction, climate change, and over-exploitation of resources.

Efforts to protect and conserve biodiversity hotspots are of utmost importance, as these regions play a vital role in maintaining global ecological balance. By understanding their distribution and significance, we can work together to ensure that these precious gems of biodiversity continue to shine brightly for generations to come.

CHAPTER 3: LIFE IN THE RAINFORESTS

EXPLORING THE LUSH CANOPIES

Rainforests, with their towering trees and verdant canopies, are among the most iconic and biodiverse ecosystems on the planet. In this section, we delve into the fascinating world of rainforest canopies, exploring the remarkable life that thrives in these lush treetop realms.

The Canopy: A Hidden World Above

The rainforest canopy, often referred to as the "treetop layer," is a rich and complex environment situated above the forest floor and below the emergent layer of the tallest trees. This region, which can extend up to 150 feet (45 meters) above the ground, is a world in itself, harboring an astonishing variety of flora and fauna.

1. Rich Biodiversity

The canopy is a biodiversity hotspot within a biodiversity hotspot. It is home to an extraordinary number of species, many of which are found nowhere else on Earth. From vibrant insects and darting birds to rare orchids and elusive mammals, the canopy's diversity is a testament to the complexity of life within rainforests.

2. Unique Adaptations

Life in the canopy demands specialized adaptations. For example, animals like tree-dwelling frogs and primates have evolved specialized limbs for navigating the treetops, while plants have developed strategies for survival, such as epiphytism (growing on other plants) and extensive root systems to reach nutrients.

3. Constant Competition

The canopy is a battleground of life and death. With limited space and abundant competition for resources, species must adapt to coexist or find unique ecological niches. This competition has led to intricate relationships and fascinating adaptations, such as canopy ants that cultivate fungus gardens.

4. Canopy Bridges and Highways

To navigate this three-dimensional environment, many canopy-dwelling animals use natural "bridges" or "highways" formed by overlapping tree branches. These pathways allow them to travel safely and efficiently through the canopy, reducing the need to descend to the forest floor.

5. Research and Discovery

The canopy has long been a subject of scientific curiosity and exploration. Canopy researchers, known as "canopy biologists" or "arborists," have developed innovative techniques like canopy walkways, cranes, and hot air balloons to study this elusive world.

Their discoveries have expanded our understanding of biodiversity and ecological interactions.

Conservation Challenges

While the canopy is a testament to the beauty and complexity of life in rainforests, it is also under threat. Deforestation, habitat fragmentation, and climate change pose significant challenges to canopy ecosystems. As these threats intensify, it becomes increasingly vital to protect these high-flying habitats.

A World Worth Protecting

Exploring the lush canopies of rainforests reveals a world of wonder and biodiversity. It underscores the importance of rainforest conservation and the need to protect these remarkable ecosystems. As we learn more about the intricacies of life in the canopy, we gain a deeper appreciation for the importance of preserving the treetop realms and the countless species that call them home.

RICHNESS OF RAINFOREST FLORA

Rainforests are not only teeming with diverse animal life but also harbor an extraordinary array of plant species. In this section, we delve into the richness of rainforest flora, exploring the remarkable adaptations, unique plant forms, and ecological importance of these botanical wonders.

1. Biodiversity Unleashed

Rainforests are often described as the "lungs of the Earth," and their lush vegetation is a testament to this nickname. These ecosystems, covering only about 6% of the Earth's land surface, are home to an estimated 50% of the world's plant and animal species. This astonishing biodiversity extends to the plant kingdom, making rainforests a treasure trove of botanical diversity.

2. Unique Adaptations

Rainforest plants have evolved an array of unique adaptations to thrive in their challenging environment. Some have developed specialized roots, like buttress roots or pneumatophores, to cope with waterlogged soils. Others exhibit epiphytism, growing on other plants to access sunlight and nutrients. Orchids, for instance, are famous epiphytes found in rainforests worldwide.

3. Towering Giants and Miniatures

One of the defining features of rainforests is the vertical stratification of vegetation. Tall emergent trees pierce the canopy, forming a lofty upper layer. Below them, the canopy layer hosts a diverse community of trees and shrubs. Beneath the canopy, the understory contains shade-tolerant plants, while the forest floor is home to ferns, mosses, and fungi.

4. Medicinal Marvels

Rainforests have long been a source of medicinal plants, providing treatments for various ailments and health conditions. Indigenous cultures have relied on the knowledge of rainforest flora for generations. Today, modern medicine continues to discover new compounds with therapeutic potential in rainforest plants.

5. Nutrient Cycling and Climate Regulation

The dense vegetation in rainforests plays a vital role in nutrient cycling and climate regulation. Plants absorb carbon dioxide from the atmosphere during photosynthesis, helping mitigate climate change. They also release water vapor through transpiration, which contributes to the formation of clouds and rainfall.

6. Mutualistic Relationships

Many rainforest plants engage in mutualistic relationships with animals. Some rely on specific pollinators, such as bats, birds, or insects, to reproduce.

In return, these animals receive nectar or fruit as a food source. These interactions are critical for both plant and animal species.

7. Conservation Challenges

Despite their ecological importance and biodiversity, rainforests are under immense pressure from deforestation, habitat fragmentation, and illegal logging.

The loss of rainforest habitat not only threatens plant species but also endangers the countless animals that rely on these ecosystems.

A Botanical Marvel

The richness of rainforest flora is a testament to the incredible diversity of life on our planet. These botanical wonders provide us with vital ecosystem services, potential medicinal breakthroughs, and a deep well of biodiversity. Protecting rainforests and their plant treasures is not only an environmental imperative but also a commitment to preserving the beauty and ecological balance of our world.

ICONIC RAINFOREST FAUNA

Rainforests, with their dense canopies and rich biodiversity, are home to some of the world's most iconic and captivating animal species. In this section, we'll embark on a virtual journey through the rainforest canopy and forest floor to encounter the fascinating and iconic fauna that call these lush jungles their home.

1. The Majestic Jaguar (Panthera onca)

The jaguar, with its powerful build and distinctive rosette-patterned coat, is the largest big cat in the Americas. This elusive predator is known for its strength and agility, often stalking its prey from the treetops before launching a precise and deadly ambush. Jaguars play a crucial role in regulating rainforest ecosystems by controlling herbivore populations.

2. The Vibrant Scarlet Macaw (Ara macao)

The rainforest canopy comes alive with the brilliant plumage of the scarlet macaw. These large, colorful parrots are renowned for their striking red, blue, and yellow feathers. Scarlet macaws are not only visually stunning but also highly intelligent, known for their impressive vocalizations and strong social bonds.

3. The Enigmatic Sloth (Family Bradypodidae)

Sloths are the epitome of life in the slow lane. These tree-dwelling mammals are famous for their leisurely pace and their distinctive appearance, with long limbs and a shaggy coat. Sloths are expert climbers and are often found hanging upside down from branches, feeding on leaves and buds.

4. The Elusive Poison Dart Frog (Family Dendrobatidae)

These tiny, brightly colored frogs are known for their striking appearance and their potent skin toxins. Indigenous peoples of the rainforest have used their toxins to poison the tips of blow darts for hunting, hence the name. The vibrant colors of poison dart frogs serve as a warning to predators about their toxicity.

5. The Diverse Primate Communities

Rainforests are primate paradises, hosting a diverse range of species, including howler monkeys, capuchins, and tamarins. These intelligent and agile creatures are often seen swinging through the trees and foraging for fruits, leaves, and insects. They also play crucial roles in seed dispersal, helping maintain the rainforest's plant diversity.

6. The Mischievous Capybara (Hydrochoerus hydrochaeris)

The capybara is the largest rodent in the world, resembling a giant guinea pig. Despite their size, these herbivorous mammals are known for their gentle and social nature. They are often seen near water sources, as they are excellent swimmers.

7. The Camouflaged Leaf-Tailed Gecko (Uroplatus spp.)

Rainforests are teeming with remarkable reptiles, including the leaf-tailed gecko. These masters of camouflage blend seamlessly with tree bark, making them nearly invisible to predators and prey alike.

Their leaf-like tails and cryptic coloration are a testament to the wonders of rainforest adaptation.

8. The Cryptic Panther Chameleon (Furcifer pardalis)

Panther chameleons are renowned for their ability to change color and their independently mobile eyes. These reptiles are true rainforest marvels, using their remarkable adaptations for communication, thermoregulation, and hunting.

Conservation Challenges and Hope

While these iconic rainforest fauna captivate our imagination, they face significant threats due to habitat loss, deforestation, and the illegal wildlife trade. Conservation efforts are critical to protect these species and the ecosystems they inhabit. Rainforests are not only home to iconic creatures but are also essential for maintaining global biodiversity, regulating climate, and providing countless ecosystem services.

Guardians of Biodiversity

The iconic rainforest fauna represent just a fraction of the incredible biodiversity found in these ecosystems. They serve as both ambassadors for rainforest conservation and crucial players in the intricate web of life within these lush jungles. Their survival is intertwined with the well-being of our planet, making their protection a global responsibility.

CHAPTER 4: DESERTS: LIFE IN EXTREME ENVIRONMENTS

ADAPTING TO ARID CONDITIONS

Arid environments, characterized by low rainfall and high evaporation rates, present one of the most challenging habitats on Earth. Yet, life has not only managed to survive but thrive in these arid conditions. In this section, we explore the remarkable adaptations that allow plants and animals to thrive in arid ecosystems.

1. Water-Saving Strategies for Plants

Plants in arid regions have developed various water-saving strategies to endure the scarcity of moisture:

Succulence: Many desert plants, such as cacti and succulents, store water in their tissues, enabling them to survive extended periods of drought.

Reduced Leaves: Some desert plants have tiny or no leaves, which helps reduce water loss through transpiration.

Deep Roots: Many arid-adapted plants have extensive root systems that reach deep into the soil to access groundwater.

Waxy Coatings: Some plants have waxy or hairy coatings on their leaves to minimize water loss through evaporation.

2. Nocturnal Activity for Animals

Many desert animals have adapted to the extreme heat of the day by becoming nocturnal. They come out to forage, hunt, and mate during the cooler nighttime hours when temperatures are more tolerable. This behavior reduces their risk of overheating and conserves energy.

3. Efficient Water Use

Desert animals have evolved highly efficient water-conservation mechanisms:

Concentrated Urine: Many desert animals produce highly concentrated urine to minimize water loss.

Body Cooling: Some animals cool themselves through behavioral adaptations, such as burrowing underground during the day to avoid the scorching sun.

4. Specialized Diets

Arid ecosystems often lack the lush vegetation found in more temperate regions. As a result, many desert animals have specialized diets, such as feeding on cacti, seeds, insects, or other animals that are adapted to arid conditions.

5. Shelter and Microhabitats

Arid environments offer numerous shelter options and microhabitats that provide relief from extreme conditions. Animals may seek refuge in burrows, rock crevices, or even beneath desert plants to escape the harsh sun and conserve moisture.

6. Long Reproductive Cycles

Reproduction in arid-adapted species is often timed to coincide with favorable conditions. Some animals reproduce only when rains are expected, ensuring that their offspring have a better chance of survival.

7. Mobility and Migration

For some species, mobility and migration are key adaptations. They move in search of food and water as conditions change, allowing them to survive in unpredictable arid landscapes.

Human Impacts and Conservation

Despite their incredible adaptations, arid ecosystems and their inhabitants are vulnerable to human activities, such as overgrazing, habitat destruction, and climate change. Conservation efforts are essential to protect these unique ecosystems and the species that rely on them.

Life's Resilience in Arid Realms

The adaptations seen in arid ecosystems highlight the remarkable resilience of life on Earth. From the unique forms of desert flora to the behavioral and physiological adaptations of desert animals, nature has found ingenious ways to not only survive but thrive in some of the harshest conditions on the planet. Understanding these adaptations not only enriches our knowledge of the natural world but also underscores the importance of conserving these fragile ecosystems.

DESERT FLORA AND FAUNA

Deserts, often characterized by their harsh, arid conditions, are home to an array of remarkable plant and animal species that have evolved to thrive in these extreme environments. In this section, we explore the unique and resilient flora and fauna of the world's deserts.

Desert Flora: Adapting to Aridity

Succulent Plants: Succulents are iconic desert plants known for their ability to store water in specialized tissues. Cacti, with their prickly exteriors and water-storing stems, are some of the most well-known succulents. Other succulent plants include agaves and aloes, which have adapted to arid conditions by reducing water loss through transpiration.

Xerophytes: Xerophytes are plants that have adapted to limited water availability. They often have small or no leaves to minimize water loss and may feature waxy coatings or hair-like structures on their surfaces to reduce evaporation. Examples include desert shrubs like sagebrush and creosote bush.

Phreatophytes: These plants have long taproots that reach deep into the soil to access groundwater. Mesquite trees and desert willows are phreatophytes that can tap into hidden water sources beneath the desert surface.

Annuals: Some desert plants are annuals, meaning they complete their entire life cycle in a single growing season, taking advantage of short periods of rain. Wildflowers, like desert marigolds and desert sunflowers, carpet the desert floor with vibrant blooms after a rainfall.

Desert Fauna: Surviving the Arid Challenge

Reptiles: Many desert reptiles have developed adaptations to conserve water and regulate their body temperature. Desert tortoises and horned lizards are excellent examples. They can store water in their bladders and use burrows or shade to avoid the scorching sun.

Birds: Desert birds are often masters of thermal regulation. Species like the roadrunner and the greater roadrunner can dissipate excess heat by panting and use behavioral adaptations like seeking shade during the hottest parts of the day.

Mammals: Desert mammals, such as kangaroo rats and camels, are adapted to both conserve and efficiently use water. Kangaroo rats, for instance, obtain most of their moisture from the seeds they eat, allowing them to live in water-scarce environments.

Arthropods: Desert arthropods, including scorpions and tarantulas, have evolved to withstand extreme temperatures and water scarcity. They often hide in burrows during the day and emerge at night to hunt for prey.

Amphibians: While amphibians are typically associated with water, some desert-dwelling species, like the spadefoot toad, have developed strategies to survive in arid environments. They can aestivate (a type of hibernation) underground for long periods and emerge to breed during brief periods of rainfall.

Conservation Challenges and Significance

Desert ecosystems face unique conservation challenges, including habitat destruction, climate change, and the impacts of human activities. Despite these challenges, desert flora and fauna play essential roles in maintaining ecological balance and are of cultural significance to indigenous peoples. Preserving these remarkable adaptations is not only crucial for biodiversity but also for understanding the resilience of life in the face of adversity.

CONSERVATION CHALLENGES IN DESERTS

Deserts, often seen as harsh and inhospitable environments, are home to unique ecosystems with their own set of conservation challenges. Despite their seeming emptiness, deserts are rich in biodiversity and play critical ecological roles. In this section, we delve into the specific conservation challenges facing desert environments.

1. Habitat Degradation and Fragmentation

Challenge: Human activities such as urbanization, agriculture, mining, and infrastructure development can lead to habitat degradation and fragmentation in deserts. These activities disrupt and destroy the fragile ecosystems that have evolved to thrive in arid conditions.

Impact: Habitat loss and fragmentation can isolate desert species, reduce genetic diversity, and limit their ability to adapt to changing conditions. It can also lead to population declines and even local extinctions.

2. Water Scarcity and Resource Extraction

Challenge: Water is a precious resource in deserts, and its scarcity is a significant conservation challenge. The extraction of groundwater for agriculture, industry, and domestic use can lead to aquifer depletion, causing springs and oases to dry up.

Impact: Water scarcity affects both desert flora and fauna. Many species have evolved to rely on these limited water sources, and their disappearance can have cascading effects on desert ecosystems.

3. Invasive Species

Challenge: Invasive species, often introduced by human activities, can outcompete and disrupt native desert species. Invasive plants, in particular, can alter desert ecosystems by monopolizing resources like water and nutrients.

Impact: Invasive species can reduce the availability of native plants and disrupt the delicate balance of desert food webs. They can also threaten the survival of rare and endemic species adapted to specific desert conditions.

4. Climate Change

Challenge: Desert ecosystems are particularly vulnerable to climate change. Rising temperatures, altered precipitation patterns, and increased droughts can exacerbate water scarcity and disrupt the timing of natural events like flowering and migration.

Impact: Climate change can push desert species to their limits, affecting their distribution and survival. Some species may be unable to adapt to rapidly changing conditions or find suitable habitats elsewhere.

5. Poaching and Illegal Wildlife Trade

Challenge: Poaching and the illegal wildlife trade can threaten desert wildlife, particularly iconic species like desert tortoises, reptiles, and rare mammals. These activities are driven by demand for exotic pets, traditional medicines, and rare animal products.

Impact: Poaching can lead to population declines and, in some cases, drive species to the brink of extinction.

The loss of charismatic species can also hinder conservation efforts by reducing public support and interest.

6. Lack of Awareness and Conservation Resources

Challenge: Desert conservation often receives less attention and fewer resources compared to other ecosystems like rainforests or coral reefs. The remote and extreme nature of desert environments can make conservation efforts more challenging.

Impact: The lack of awareness and resources can hinder research, monitoring, and conservation initiatives, making it difficult to protect desert ecosystems and the species that depend on them.

Conservation Efforts and Hope

Despite these challenges, there is hope for desert conservation. Efforts are underway to protect and restore desert habitats, raise awareness about the importance of these ecosystems, and implement sustainable practices that minimize the impact of human activities. Desert conservation not only preserves unique biodiversity but also contributes to the global effort to protect our planet's natural heritage and combat climate change.

CHAPTER 5: CORAL REEFS: JEWELS OF THE OCEAN

THE UNDERWATER WONDERLAND

Beneath the shimmering surface of Earth's oceans lies a realm of unparalleled beauty and wonder. The underwater world, often referred to as the "underwater wonderland," is a mesmerizing and diverse ecosystem that covers over 70% of our planet. In this exploration, we dive deep into this mysterious realm to discover its breathtaking inhabitants and the critical role it plays in sustaining life on Earth.

1. A Vast and Mysterious Domain

The world's oceans encompass vast expanses, from the sunlit shallows to the crushing depths of the abyssal plains. This immense underwater world is home to an astonishing variety of life forms, many of which remain undiscovered and unnamed by science.

2. Biodiversity Beyond Imagination

The biodiversity of the oceans is staggering. From the smallest plankton to the largest whales, marine life exhibits an incredible range of shapes, colors, and behaviors.

Coral reefs alone are estimated to host a quarter of all marine species, making them the rainforests of the sea.

3. Coral Reefs: Cities of the Ocean

Coral reefs are some of the most diverse and productive ecosystems on Earth. These underwater cities provide shelter and sustenance to countless species, including vibrant coral polyps, colorful fish, and apex predators like sharks.

4. Ocean Giants and Migrations

The oceans are home to awe-inspiring giants like the blue whale, the largest animal to have ever existed on Earth. Many marine species undertake epic migrations, crossing thousands of miles, from sea turtles nesting on remote beaches to humpback whales traveling between feeding and breeding grounds.

5. Adaptations to Extreme Environments

Life in the underwater wonderland has led to remarkable adaptations. Deep-sea creatures, such as anglerfish with bioluminescent lures and giant tube worms near hydrothermal vents, thrive in extreme conditions of darkness, pressure, and heat.

6. The Role of Oceans in Climate Regulation

Oceans play a crucial role in regulating Earth's climate. They absorb vast amounts of heat and carbon dioxide, helping to stabilize global temperatures and mitigate the impacts of climate change. Phytoplankton, microscopic marine plants, produce more oxygen than all the world's forests combined, making them the lungs of the planet.

7. Conservation Imperatives

Despite their immense importance, the oceans face unprecedented challenges, including overfishing, habitat destruction, pollution, and the acidification caused by excess carbon dioxide absorption. These threats endanger marine life and disrupt the delicate balance of ocean ecosystems.

Hope for the Future

Efforts to protect and conserve the underwater wonderland are underway worldwide. Marine protected areas, sustainable fisheries practices, and international agreements like the Paris Agreement and the United Nations Sustainable Development Goal 14 (Life Below Water) aim to safeguard the oceans for future generations.

The underwater wonderland reminds us of the interconnectedness of all life on Earth. It is a source of inspiration, scientific discovery, and endless fascination. By understanding, respecting, and actively conserving this remarkable realm, we can ensure that the oceans continue to thrive and sustain life on our blue planet for generations to come.

Coral Species and Their Importance

Coral reefs, often referred to as the "rainforests of the sea," are among the most diverse and vital ecosystems on Earth. They are constructed by countless species of corals, which are not only mesmerizing in their beauty but also play a crucial role in sustaining life in the oceans. In this exploration, we dive into the world of coral species and their immense ecological importance.

1. The Diversity of Coral Species

Coral reefs are built by a vast array of coral species, each with its unique characteristics and contributions to the ecosystem. Some of the most well-known types of corals include:

Hard Corals (Scleractinia): These corals are the primary reef builders, forming the sturdy calcium carbonate skeletons that provide the framework for reefs. Examples include brain corals, staghorn corals, and elkhorn corals.

Soft Corals (Alcyonacea): Soft corals, as the name suggests, lack the hard skeletons of their cousins. They are known for their vibrant, flexible polyps and include sea fans, sea whips, and leather corals.

Fire Corals (Milleporidae): Fire corals, although not true corals, are often mistaken for them due to their appearance. They are actually hydrozoans and possess a painful sting.

Black Corals (Antipatharia): Black corals are renowned for their striking black or dark brown skeletons. They are found in deep waters and can live for centuries.

2. The Ecosystem Engineers

Coral species are the architects of coral reefs. They secrete calcium carbonate, building intricate structures that provide habitat, protection, and feeding grounds for an astounding variety of marine life. The nooks and crannies within coral reefs offer refuge to numerous fish, invertebrates, and algae.

3. Biodiversity Hotspots

Coral reefs are renowned for their unparalleled biodiversity. Although they cover less than 1% of the ocean floor, they support about 25% of all marine species. This includes not only corals themselves but also an astonishing range of fish, crustaceans, mollusks, and other creatures.

4. Economic and Ecological Value

Coral reefs have significant economic and ecological importance:

Fisheries: Many commercially important fish species rely on coral reefs as breeding and nursery grounds. Healthy reefs contribute to sustainable fisheries and food security for coastal communities.

Tourism: Coral reefs attract millions of tourists each year, generating revenue for coastal economies. The beauty of these ecosystems, with their vibrant corals and colorful marine life, makes them prime destinations for divers and snorkelers.

Coastal Protection: Coral reefs act as natural barriers, protecting coastlines from erosion and storm surges.

They reduce the impact of powerful waves and help mitigate the effects of climate change.

5. Threats to Coral Reefs

Coral species and the reefs they create are under severe threat from a range of human-induced stressors, including:

Climate Change: Rising sea temperatures cause coral bleaching, a phenomenon where corals expel the symbiotic algae that provide them with nutrients and color. Repeated bleaching events can lead to coral mortality.

Ocean Acidification: Increased carbon dioxide levels in the atmosphere are absorbed by the oceans, leading to ocean acidification. This can weaken coral skeletons and inhibit their growth.

Pollution: Land-based pollution, including runoff of chemicals, sewage, and plastic debris, can smother corals and disrupt their delicate ecosystems.

Overfishing: Unsustainable fishing practices can deplete fish populations that help maintain the health of coral reefs.

Conservation Efforts

Efforts to protect coral reefs and their resident coral species include the establishment of marine protected areas, sustainable fisheries management, and initiatives to reduce greenhouse gas emissions. Public awareness and education also play a vital role in promoting the conservation of these invaluable ecosystems.

Coral species are the architects of coral reefs, creating underwater wonderlands that harbor incredible biodiversity and provide essential services to our planet. Protecting these fragile ecosystems is not just a matter of conservation but also an investment in the well-being of coastal communities and the preservation of Earth's natural beauty.

THREATS TO CORAL REEFS AND CONSERVATION EFFORTS

Coral reefs, vibrant and diverse ecosystems, are facing unprecedented challenges that threaten their very existence. As one of the most biologically rich and economically valuable habitats on Earth, the conservation of coral reefs is crucial. In this exploration, we'll delve into the threats facing coral reefs and the ongoing efforts to protect and preserve these invaluable underwater wonders.

Threats to Coral Reefs

Climate Change:

Coral Bleaching: Rising sea temperatures stress coral colonies, causing them to expel the symbiotic algae (zooxanthellae) that provide them with nutrients and color. This leads to coral bleaching, making corals more susceptible to disease and death.

Ocean Acidification: Increased levels of carbon dioxide in the atmosphere are absorbed by seawater, leading to ocean acidification. This can weaken coral skeletons, making them more vulnerable to physical damage.

Pollution:

Land-Based Pollution: Runoff from agriculture, deforestation, and urban areas carries sediment, chemicals, and nutrients into coastal waters. This pollution can smother corals, promote algal growth, and disrupt the delicate balance of reef ecosystems.

Marine Debris: Plastics and other debris can damage corals, introduce toxins, and entangle marine life. Lost fishing gear, such as nets and traps, can cause physical harm to reefs.

Overfishing and Destructive Fishing Practices:

Overfishing of herbivorous fish species can lead to an overgrowth of algae, which can smother corals and prevent new coral recruits from settling.

Destructive fishing practices, such as dynamite fishing and cyanide fishing, can physically damage coral reefs and disrupt their ecological integrity.

Coastal Development:

Coastal construction, dredging, and the destruction of mangroves and seagrass beds can lead to increased sedimentation and nutrient runoff, harming nearby coral reefs.

Conservation Efforts

Marine Protected Areas (MPAs): Establishing and effectively managing MPAs can provide refuge for marine life and reduce the impact of human activities on coral reefs. MPAs can also serve as important research and monitoring sites.

Sustainable Fisheries Management: Implementing and enforcing fishing regulations, such as size limits, catch quotas, and gear restrictions, can help restore fish populations and maintain the ecological balance of coral reefs.

Coral Restoration and Reef Resilience: Conservation organizations and scientists are working to restore damaged coral reefs by cultivating resilient coral species and replanting them onto degraded reefs.

Climate Change Mitigation: Efforts to reduce greenhouse gas emissions are essential to combat rising sea temperatures and ocean acidification. International agreements like the Paris Agreement aim to limit global warming.

Public Awareness and Education: Raising awareness about the importance of coral reefs and the threats they face is vital. Education campaigns can promote responsible tourism, sustainable seafood choices, and the reduction of single-use plastics.

Community Involvement: Engaging local communities in reef conservation efforts can lead to more effective and sustainable practices. Empowering communities to protect their natural resources is key to long-term success.

Coral reefs are not only breathtakingly beautiful but also vital for the health of our oceans and the livelihoods of millions of people. The threats they face are complex and interconnected, but concerted conservation efforts at local, national, and global levels can help safeguard these precious underwater ecosystems for future generations.

Coral reefs are resilient, but they need our help to overcome the unprecedented challenges they currently face.

CHAPTER 6: MOUNTAINS: HIGH ALTITUDE HOTSPOTS

THE BREATHTAKING DIVERSITY OF MOUNTAIN ECOSYSTEMS

Mountain ecosystems, characterized by their towering peaks, steep slopes, and varying altitudes, are among the most diverse and captivating environments on Earth. From the lush valleys to the rocky summits, these high-rise habitats are home to a remarkable array of flora and fauna. In this exploration, we ascend into the world of mountain ecosystems to discover their breathtaking diversity and ecological significance.

1. Altitudinal Variation

One of the defining features of mountain ecosystems is the dramatic change in climate and vegetation with altitude. This altitudinal variation gives rise to distinct zones or "life belts," each with its unique flora and fauna. These zones often include the following:

Montane Forests: Found at lower altitudes, these forests are home to a variety of trees, shrubs, and animals, including deer, bears, and a rich diversity of birds.

Subalpine Zone: As you ascend, the landscape transitions to subalpine meadows and coniferous forests. This zone is known for its colorful wildflowers, marmots, and mountain goats.

Alpine Tundra: At even higher elevations, the vegetation becomes sparse, and you enter the alpine tundra, where hardy plants like mosses, lichens, and low-growing herbs thrive. Here, animals like pikas and ptarmigans are adapted to extreme cold.

Rock and Ice: The highest reaches of mountains are often barren, dominated by rock and ice. Yet, even in these seemingly inhospitable environments, life persists. Microscopic organisms can be found in the ice, and alpine birds, such as the snow finch, visit these areas.

2. Unique Adaptations

Mountain flora and fauna have evolved remarkable adaptations to cope with the challenges of high-altitude living. These include:

Thick Fur and Feathers: Many mountain animals have thick fur or feathers to insulate against the cold.

Snow leopards, for example, are adapted to the frigid temperatures of the Himalayan and Central Asian mountains.

Short Growing Seasons: Plants in high-altitude environments must make the most of short growing seasons. They often have rapid growth patterns during the brief warm periods.

Specialized Diets: Animals in mountain ecosystems often have specialized diets, such as grazing on alpine grasses or foraging for insects in rocky crevices.

3. Water Sources and Ecosystem Services

Mountain ecosystems are crucial sources of freshwater for downstream communities and agriculture. Melting snow and glaciers feed into rivers that sustain life in lower elevations. These ecosystems also play a vital role in regulating global climate patterns.

4. Conservation Challenges

Mountain ecosystems, despite their isolation, are not immune to human impacts:

Climate Change: Rising temperatures in mountain regions are causing glaciers to melt, affecting water availability and threatening species adapted to cold environments.

Habitat Destruction: Infrastructure development, mining, and deforestation in mountainous areas can lead to habitat destruction and fragmentation.

Tourism Pressure: Tourism can bring economic benefits but also contribute to habitat degradation and pollution if not managed sustainably.

Conservation Efforts

Efforts to protect mountain ecosystems include the establishment of protected areas, sustainable land-use practices, and initiatives to mitigate climate change. These conservation actions are essential not only for preserving biodiversity but also for securing vital freshwater resources and ensuring the continued well-being of mountain communities.

Mountain ecosystems are a testament to the resilience and adaptability of life on Earth. From the towering peaks to the rugged valleys, these high-rise habitats host a stunning variety of species and play a critical role in maintaining our planet's ecological balance. As we admire the breathtaking diversity of mountain ecosystems, let us also commit to their conservation, recognizing their intrinsic value and the services they provide to both nature and humanity.

UNIQUE MOUNTAIN FLORA AND FAUNA

Mountain ecosystems, with their rugged terrain and dramatic changes in altitude, are havens for unique and specialized flora and fauna. These high-altitude habitats are characterized by a rich tapestry of life that has adapted to the challenges of living in extreme environments. In this exploration, we ascend into the world of mountain ecosystems to discover the extraordinary and often endemic species that call these regions home.

1. Alpine Flora: A World of Tiny Treasures

Alpine zones, found at high elevations above the tree line, are home to an array of exquisite and hardy plants. These florae have evolved remarkable adaptations to cope with cold temperatures, intense sunlight, and short growing seasons. Some notable examples include:

Edelweiss (Leontopodium alpinum): Known for its white, star-shaped blooms, the edelweiss is an iconic alpine flower. It's often associated with rugged mountain landscapes and has become a symbol of alpinism.

Alpine Gentians: These vibrant blue and purple flowers are prized for their striking color and are found in mountain regions around the world.

Cushion Plants: Some alpine plants grow in compact, cushion-like formations that provide insulation from the cold and protection from strong winds. These cushions often harbor other specialized species, including insects.

2. Cold-Adapted Fauna: Survivors of the Chill

Mountain ecosystems are home to a range of unique and well-adapted animal species. These creatures have developed a variety of strategies to thrive in the cold and rugged mountain terrain. Notable examples include:

Snow Leopard (Panthera uncia): These elusive big cats are perfectly adapted to the harsh conditions of the Himalayas and Central Asian mountains. Their thick fur and spotted coats provide camouflage in snowy landscapes.

Pika (Ochotona spp.): Pikas are small, herbivorous mammals related to rabbits.

They are active year-round and have adapted to cold environments by creating hay piles to sustain them through winter.

Alpine Ibex (Capra ibex): These powerful, horned goats are renowned for their climbing abilities and can be found scaling steep cliffs and rocky outcrops in search of food and safety.

3. Endemic Species: The Masters of Isolation

Mountain ecosystems often harbor species found nowhere else on Earth, known as endemics. These species have evolved in isolation over long periods, resulting in unique adaptations and genetic diversity. Some examples include:

The Himalayan Monal (Lophophorus impejanus): This stunning bird, known for its iridescent plumage, is found in the Himalayas and surrounding mountain ranges.

Mount Kinabalu Pitcher Plant (Nepenthes rajah): The pitcher plants of Mount Kinabalu in Borneo are among the largest carnivorous plants in the world.

They have evolved to capture and digest insects in nutrient-poor soils.

Madagascar's High-Altitude Chameleons: Madagascar's montane ecosystems are home to a variety of chameleon species, each uniquely adapted to its specific habitat and elevational range.

4. Conservation Challenges and Efforts

Mountain ecosystems and their unique flora and fauna face a range of threats, including climate change, habitat destruction, and unsustainable tourism. Conservation efforts are crucial to protect these fragile habitats and the species that inhabit them. Initiatives include the creation of protected areas, sustainable land-use practices, and research to better understand and preserve high-altitude biodiversity.

Mountain ecosystems offer a glimpse into the incredible adaptability and diversity of life on our planet. These regions are not only biological treasures but also vital sources of fresh water and ecological services. As we celebrate the unique flora and fauna of mountain environments, let us also commit to their conservation, ensuring that these high-altitude wonders continue to inspire and thrive for generations to come.

CLIMATE CHANGE AND MOUNTAIN BIODIVERSITY

Mountain ecosystems, with their unique flora and fauna, are particularly vulnerable to the impacts of climate change. Rising temperatures, altered precipitation patterns, and shifting snowmelt are transforming these high-altitude habitats at an alarming rate. In this exploration, we delve into the intricate relationship between climate change and mountain biodiversity and the challenges these ecosystems face.

1. Temperature Increases:

Altitudinal Shifts: As temperatures rise, many mountain species are moving upslope in search of cooler conditions. This uphill migration can lead to competition for limited resources and potential loss of habitat for species already occupying higher elevations.

Threats to Cold-Adapted Species: Species adapted to cold environments, such as snow leopards and alpine plants, are at risk as their specialized habitats shrink.

These species may face increased vulnerability to diseases and predators as warming progresses.

2. Altered Precipitation Patterns:

Changes in Water Availability: Mountain ecosystems are often dependent on seasonal snow and ice melt for a consistent water supply. Altered precipitation patterns can disrupt this delicate balance, affecting not only plant growth but also the availability of water for wildlife.

Impact on Alpine Flora: Alpine plants, which have adapted to low water availability, may struggle to survive in a changing climate with irregular rainfall patterns. This can lead to reduced food sources for herbivores and ecosystem disruptions.

3. Increased Extreme Weather Events:

Landslides and Erosion: Extreme weather events, including heavy rainfall and rapid snowmelt, can trigger landslides and erosion in mountainous regions. These events can bury habitats and disrupt ecosystems.

Avalanches: Warmer temperatures can lead to more unstable snowpacks, increasing the frequency and severity of avalanches, which can impact both wildlife and human communities.

4. Glacier Retreat:

Water Source Disruption: Glacier retreat affects not only the availability of freshwater downstream but also the unique ecosystems that rely on glacial meltwater. Species like glacier fleas and stoneflies, adapted to cold, glacial-fed streams, may face habitat loss.

5. Conservation Challenges and Efforts:

Habitat Fragmentation: Climate change can lead to fragmented habitats as species move to higher elevations. Conservation efforts must consider the connectivity of these fragmented areas to maintain genetic diversity and allow for species migration.

Protected Areas: Establishing and expanding protected areas in mountain regions can provide refuge for vulnerable species. These areas serve as climate refugia, where species can persist in suitable conditions.

Community Engagement: Collaborating with local communities that depend on mountain ecosystems for their livelihoods is essential. Sustainable land-use practices, including reduced grazing pressure and reforestation, can help mitigate the impacts of climate change.

Mountain biodiversity is under immense pressure due to climate change. These high-altitude ecosystems, often seen as remote and pristine, are not immune to the global challenges of a warming world. Protecting mountain biodiversity is not only crucial for preserving unique species but also for ensuring the continued availability of freshwater resources and ecosystem services. Addressing climate change and its impacts on mountain ecosystems is a global imperative that requires international cooperation, conservation efforts, and sustainable practices to safeguard these vital habitats for future generations.

CHAPTER 7: ISLANDS: EVOLUTIONARY LABORATORIES

ISLANDS AS NATURAL EXPERIMENTS

Islands, often remote and isolated, have long fascinated scientists and explorers alike. These landmasses, surrounded by oceanic barriers, offer unique opportunities to study and understand ecological and evolutionary processes. Islands are like natural experiments in evolution, where the isolation and selective pressures have led to the development of extraordinary biodiversity and adaptations. In this exploration, we'll dive into the concept of islands as natural experiments and discover the evolutionary wonders they hold.

1. Isolation and Speciation:

Islands, being isolated from the mainland, provide a setting where species can evolve independently. Over time, this isolation can lead to the development of new species through a process called speciation. The absence of competition and the presence of unique ecological niches often result in rapid and remarkable adaptations.

2. Adaptive Radiation:

Islands are often hotspots for adaptive radiation, where a single ancestral species diversifies into multiple species, each adapted to different ecological niches. The Galápagos Islands, famously studied by Charles Darwin, are a classic example of adaptive radiation. Darwin's finches, with their diverse beak shapes and feeding habits, illustrate how species can rapidly adapt to their environments.

3. Gigantism and Dwarfism:

Islands are known for their extraordinary examples of gigantism and dwarfism. Limited resources and the absence of natural predators can lead to the evolution of giant species, such as the Komodo dragon of Indonesia. Conversely, islands can also be home to dwarfed species, like the miniature elephants of Sicily and Malta. These extreme size differences are a testament to the power of island evolution.

4. Unusual Behaviors:

Isolation on islands can lead to the development of unique behaviors not seen on the mainland. For example, the kakapo of New Zealand is a nocturnal, flightless parrot that has evolved to fill a niche as a ground-dwelling herbivore. Its peculiar behavior is a result of the absence of mammalian predators on the island.

5. Vulnerability to Extinction:

While islands are cradles of biodiversity, they are also fragile ecosystems. Limited land area, invasive species, and human activities make island species particularly vulnerable to extinction. Many island species have tragically disappeared or are critically endangered due to habitat destruction and the introduction of non-native species.

6. Conservation Significance:

Islands play a crucial role in global conservation efforts. The unique biodiversity found on islands makes them a priority for conservation action. Protecting island ecosystems helps preserve not only endemic species but also the broader biodiversity of our planet.

Islands, as natural experiments in evolution, continue to unlock the mysteries of life on Earth. They provide invaluable insights into how species adapt, diversify, and coexist in isolated environments. However, islands also serve as a stark reminder of the urgent need for conservation and responsible stewardship of these fragile ecosystems. As we explore the wonders of island evolution, let us also commit to preserving these unique environments and the extraordinary life they nurture.

ISLAND BIOGEOGRAPHY

Island biogeography is a field of study that explores the ecological and evolutionary processes shaping the distribution, diversity, and dynamics of life on islands. Islands, often isolated and distinct from the mainland, serve as natural laboratories for understanding fundamental principles of biodiversity and conservation. In this exploration, we delve into the fascinating world of island biogeography and its key concepts.

1. Island Characteristics:

Islands come in various sizes, from tiny islets to large landmasses. They can be oceanic, formed by geological processes like volcanic eruptions, or continental, once part of a larger landmass but separated by rising sea levels. The size, isolation, age, and habitat diversity of an island profoundly influence its biogeography.

2. Species Diversity on Islands:

Islands can exhibit strikingly high levels of endemism, with species found nowhere else on Earth. This phenomenon occurs due to isolation, limited gene flow with the mainland, and the potential for rapid speciation. Islands also often harbor fewer species than nearby mainland areas, a principle known as the "species-area relationship," which states that larger islands generally have more species.

3. Immigration and Extinction:

Islands' isolation leads to the concept of immigration and extinction dynamics. Species can colonize islands, adding to their biodiversity. However, due to limited resources and increased competition, some species may go extinct on islands. The balance between immigration and extinction governs species richness on an island.

4. Equilibrium Theory of Island Biogeography:

Developed by Robert MacArthur and E.O. Wilson in the 1960s, the equilibrium theory of island biogeography proposes that species richness on an island reaches a dynamic equilibrium, balancing colonization and extinction rates. Larger islands with fewer extinctions and higher immigration rates tend to maintain more diverse communities.

5. Island Size and Distance:

Two key factors influencing species diversity on islands are size and distance from the mainland. Larger islands offer more habitat diversity, reducing competition and allowing more species to coexist. Islands closer to the mainland generally have higher immigration rates, leading to higher species richness.

6. Conservation Implications:

Island biogeography has significant implications for conservation. Fragile island ecosystems, often home to endemic and endangered species, are vulnerable to habitat loss, invasive species, and climate change.

Understanding the principles of island biogeography can guide conservation efforts, such as the creation of protected areas and the management of invasive species.

7. Case Studies:

Several iconic islands have been integral to the study of island biogeography:

The Galápagos Islands: Charles Darwin's observations on these islands played a pivotal role in the development of evolutionary theory. They are renowned for their unique species, including the Galápagos tortoises and finches.

Hawaiian Islands: Isolation and volcanic diversity have led to a profusion of unique species in Hawaii, including the Hawaiian honeycreepers and the silver sword plant.

Madagascar: This massive island off the eastern coast of Africa is a biodiversity hotspot with numerous endemic species, such as lemurs, chameleons, and baobab trees.

Island biogeography offers profound insights into the complex dynamics of biodiversity, species colonization, and extinction. It underscores the critical importance of conserving island ecosystems, which are not only natural wonders but also laboratories for understanding the broader principles of ecology and evolution. By safeguarding these unique environments, we can protect not only island life but also the invaluable lessons it teaches us about the world's biological diversity.

CHALLENGES OF ISLAND CONSERVATION

Islands, with their unique ecosystems and often isolated biodiversity, are havens for both endemic species and ecological wonders. However, they also face a host of conservation challenges that threaten these fragile paradises. In this exploration, we delve into the complex and pressing issues surrounding island conservation.

1. Invasive Species:

One of the most significant threats to island ecosystems is the introduction of invasive species. These non-native plants and animals can outcompete, prey upon, or disrupt the native species, often leading to declines or extinctions. Invasive species arrive on islands through human activities such as trade, tourism, and accidental transport.

2. Habitat Loss and Degradation:

Islands are often developed for agriculture, tourism, and urbanization. As human populations grow and economies expand, natural habitats are lost or fragmented, diminishing available resources and space for native species.

3. Climate Change:

Rising global temperatures and sea levels affect islands in numerous ways. For low-lying atolls and coastal islands, sea-level rise threatens to inundate habitats and freshwater sources. Warmer temperatures can alter rainfall patterns and increase the frequency of extreme weather events, impacting both terrestrial and marine ecosystems.

4. Pollution:

Pollution from land-based sources, including runoff of agricultural chemicals and wastewater, can harm island ecosystems. Coral reefs, in particular, are susceptible to pollution, which can lead to coral bleaching and reduced water quality.

5. Overexploitation:

Unsustainable fishing practices can deplete marine resources around islands, affecting not only the species being harvested but also the broader marine food web. The loss of keystone species can have cascading effects throughout the ecosystem.

6. Limited Resources and Expertise:

Many islands have limited financial and human resources for conservation efforts. Smaller and less economically developed islands may struggle to implement effective conservation measures or adequately enforce regulations.

7. Fragmentation and Isolation:

Islands are often isolated from the mainland, making it difficult for species to recolonize after local extinctions. This isolation can lead to a lack of genetic diversity and increase the vulnerability of island species.

8. Conservation Conflicts:

Conservation goals sometimes conflict with the economic interests of island communities. For example, restrictions on fishing or tourism may be necessary for conservation, but they can strain local livelihoods.

Conservation Solutions:

Addressing the challenges of island conservation requires a multi-faceted approach:

Invasive Species Management: Strategies to control or eradicate invasive species are crucial. These efforts may involve habitat restoration, biosecurity measures, and ongoing monitoring.

Habitat Restoration: Restoring degraded habitats, reforestation, and creating protected areas can help safeguard native species and ecosystems.

Climate Change Adaptation: Preparing for climate change impacts, such as rising sea levels, involves both mitigation and adaptation efforts. Coastal defenses and habitat restoration can protect against erosion and habitat loss.

Community Engagement: Engaging local communities in conservation efforts can lead to more sustainable practices and better outcomes for both people and nature.

International Cooperation: Given that many islands are part of larger archipelagos or regions, international cooperation is vital for effective conservation. Agreements and partnerships can help protect shared resources.

Island conservation is a complex and urgent endeavor. The preservation of these unique ecosystems not only protects biodiversity but also ensures the well-being of local communities and the long-term health of our planet. Balancing the delicate balance between conservation and human needs is a challenge, but it is essential for safeguarding the fragile paradises that islands represent.

CHAPTER 8: HOTSPOTS OF AFRICA: FROM SAVANNAS TO JUNGLES

AFRICAN BIODIVERSITY RICHES

Africa, often referred to as the cradle of humanity, is not only the world's second-largest continent but also one of the most biodiverse regions on Earth. Its diverse landscapes, from lush rainforests to arid deserts, provide habitats for an astounding array of flora and fauna. In this exploration, we'll delve into the unparalleled biodiversity riches that Africa harbors and their significance for our planet.

1. Breathtaking Ecosystem Diversity:

Africa's vast expanse encompasses a remarkable range of ecosystems:

Rainforests: The Congo Basin and the West African rainforests are among the world's most biodiverse habitats, home to countless plant and animal species, including gorillas, chimpanzees, and myriad bird species.

Savannas: Iconic African landscapes, savannas teem with wildlife, from the "Big Five" (elephants, lions, leopards, rhinoceroses, and buffaloes) to countless grazers, predators, and avian species.

Deserts: The Sahara Desert in North Africa, the Kalahari in the south, and the Namib along the southwestern coast are deserts of stunning beauty and unique life forms, adapted to harsh arid conditions.

Mountains: Africa boasts a range of mountains, including the Ethiopian Highlands and the Rwenzori Mountains, which harbor unique flora and fauna adapted to high-altitude environments.

2. Rich Faunal Diversity:

Africa is renowned for its spectacular wildlife:

Big Five: The term "Big Five" was coined by big-game hunters and includes some of Africa's most iconic species: elephants, lions, leopards, rhinoceroses, and buffaloes.

Primates: Africa is the continent of primates, with various species of chimpanzees, gorillas, baboons, and lemurs inhabiting different regions.

Birds: It's a birdwatcher's paradise with over 2,300 bird species, including ostriches, eagles, vultures, and brightly colored passerines.

Endemic Species: Many species are found only in Africa, such as the okapi, a forest-dwelling relative of the giraffe, and the African penguin.

3. Critical Ecosystem Services:

African ecosystems provide essential services to both local communities and the global environment:

Freshwater Resources: The continent's rivers, including the Nile, Congo, and Niger, supply water to millions of people and support diverse aquatic life.

Agriculture and Livelihoods: African biodiversity underpins agricultural productivity, food security, and livelihoods for countless communities.

Carbon Storage: Forests, savannas, and wetlands in Africa play a crucial role in storing carbon and mitigating climate change.

4. Conservation Challenges:

Africa's biodiversity faces a range of challenges:

Habitat Loss: Deforestation, urbanization, and agriculture continue to encroach upon natural habitats, threatening many species.

Poaching and Wildlife Trade: Poaching for ivory, rhino horn, and bushmeat remains a significant threat to iconic species.

Climate Change: Changing weather patterns and increased temperatures affect both species and ecosystems.

5. Conservation Efforts:

Numerous conservation organizations, governments, and local communities are working tirelessly to protect Africa's biodiversity. Initiatives include the establishment of protected areas, anti-poaching efforts, community-based conservation, and sustainable land-use practices.

Africa's biodiversity riches are a global treasure, supporting unique ecosystems, sustaining local communities, and offering a glimpse into the intricate tapestry of life on Earth. The conservation of Africa's natural heritage is not only vital for the continent but also crucial for maintaining the planet's ecological balance and safeguarding the future of countless species.

Preserving Africa's biodiversity is a shared responsibility that requires international cooperation and sustainable practices to ensure the survival of these natural treasures for generations to come.

THE GREAT RIFT VALLEY AND ITS SIGNIFICANCE

The Great Rift Valley, often simply referred to as the Rift Valley, is one of the most awe-inspiring geological features on our planet. Stretching over 6,000 kilometers (3,700 miles) from the Middle East to Eastern Africa, it is a colossal trench that bears witness to the dynamic forces shaping Earth's surface. In this exploration, we delve into the significance of the Great Rift Valley, both from a geological and a human perspective.

1. Geological Formation:

The Great Rift Valley is the result of the complex interactions between tectonic plates beneath the Earth's surface. It is primarily formed by the divergence of two major plates:

African Plate: The African Plate, which comprises the African continent, is slowly splitting into two parts along the East African Rift, a continental rift zone that runs through the eastern side of the continent.

Somalian Plate: To the east of the East African Rift, the Somalian Plate is separating from the African Plate, causing the valley to gradually widen.

The geological forces at play in the Rift Valley have resulted in a variety of stunning landscapes, including deep valleys, high plateaus, volcanoes, and extensive lakes.

2. Lakes of the Rift Valley:

The Great Rift Valley is renowned for its numerous lakes, many of which are remarkable in their own right:

Lake Victoria: Africa's largest freshwater lake, Lake Victoria, is a vital resource for the surrounding region. It is a hub of biodiversity and supports numerous species of fish.

Lake Tanganyika: This ancient lake is not only the deepest in Africa but also the second-deepest in the world, containing unique and endemic aquatic life.

Lake Turkana: Often referred to as the "Jade Sea" due to its stunning blue-green color, Lake Turkana is the world's largest desert lake and harbors various archaeological and paleontological treasures.

3. Biodiversity and Human History:

The diverse landscapes and abundant water sources of the Rift Valley have played a crucial role in shaping both the natural world and human history:

Biodiversity: The Rift Valley is home to a rich array of plant and animal species, many of which are found nowhere else on Earth. This biodiversity hotspot is a testament to the evolutionary processes at work in the region.

Human Evolution: The Rift Valley is often referred to as the "Cradle of Humanity" because it is believed to be the birthplace of our species. Numerous hominid fossils have been discovered here, shedding light on our evolutionary history.

Cultural Significance: The Rift Valley has been inhabited by diverse cultures and civilizations for millennia.

It has been a source of inspiration for art, literature, and folklore, contributing to the rich tapestry of human heritage.

4. Conservation and Challenges:

Despite its geological and cultural significance, the Rift Valley faces several conservation challenges:

Habitat Destruction: Increasing human populations, deforestation, and unsustainable land use threaten the region's natural habitats.

Water Management: The management of water resources in the Rift Valley is a complex issue, with competing demands for agriculture, industry, and conservation.

Climate Change: The effects of climate change, including altered rainfall patterns and temperature increases, pose additional challenges to the region's ecosystems and communities.

The Great Rift Valley is a living testament to the Earth's geological processes and a crucible of human history and biodiversity.

Its significance transcends borders and disciplines, making it a treasure trove of scientific knowledge, cultural heritage, and natural wonders. As we continue to explore and understand this remarkable geological masterpiece, it is imperative that we also work together to protect and conserve its ecological and cultural richness for future generations.

CONSERVATION INITIATIVES IN AFRICAN HOTSPOTS

Africa is home to some of the world's most remarkable biodiversity hotspots, regions teeming with unique and often endangered species. These ecological treasures face a range of threats, from habitat loss to poaching, underscoring the urgent need for conservation efforts. In this exploration, we delve into the initiatives aimed at protecting Africa's biodiversity hotspots and preserving the continent's natural heritage.

1. The Importance of Biodiversity Hotspots:

Biodiversity hotspots are areas characterized by exceptionally high levels of species diversity and endemism. African hotspots are no exception, boasting unique ecosystems and iconic species. These regions provide essential ecosystem services, support local livelihoods, and contribute to global biodiversity.

2. Key African Biodiversity Hotspots:

Africa hosts several biodiversity hotspots, including:

Cape Floristic Region: Located in South Africa, this hotspot is renowned for its extraordinary plant diversity, including the iconic fynbos vegetation.

Eastern Afromontane: Spanning from the Ethiopian Highlands to the mountains of southern Africa, this hotspot harbors diverse montane ecosystems.

Madagascar and the Indian Ocean Islands: Madagascar alone is a biodiversity hotspot, known for its endemic lemurs, chameleons, and diverse flora.

Guinean Forests of West Africa: This hotspot spans several West African countries and contains dense rainforests with a wealth of species.

3. Conservation Initiatives:

Numerous conservation initiatives and organizations are dedicated to protecting these hotspots:

Protected Areas: Establishing and managing protected areas is a cornerstone of conservation efforts.

These areas provide safe havens for wildlife and serve as centers for scientific research and ecotourism.

Community-Based Conservation: Engaging local communities in conservation efforts is crucial. Sustainable land-use practices and community-managed reserves can help reduce pressure on natural resources.

Anti-Poaching Efforts: Many hotspots are plagued by poaching, particularly of iconic species like elephants and rhinos. Anti-poaching units and law enforcement efforts are critical to combat this threat.

Research and Monitoring: Scientific research is essential for understanding hotspots' unique ecosystems and monitoring changes over time. This knowledge informs conservation strategies.

Conservation NGOs: Organizations like the African Wildlife Foundation, Conservation International, and the World-Wide Fund for Nature (WWF) work in collaboration with governments and local partners to protect hotspots.

4. Success Stories:

There have been notable successes in African hotspot conservation:

Gorilla Conservation: Conservation efforts in the Virunga Mountains of East Africa have led to significant increases in mountain gorilla populations.

Madagascar's Lemurs: Conservation programs have helped stabilize lemur populations and protect their habitats in Madagascar.

Cape Floristic Region: Conservation efforts have led to the recovery of several endangered plant species in this hotspot.

5. Ongoing Challenges:

Despite progress, conservation in African hotspots faces persistent challenges:

Habitat Loss: The expansion of agriculture, infrastructure development, and logging continue to threaten critical habitats.

Poverty and Human-Wildlife Conflict: Many hotspot regions struggle with poverty, and human-wildlife conflict can undermine conservation efforts.

Climate Change: Shifts in temperature and rainfall patterns impact hotspot ecosystems and species.

Conservation initiatives in African hotspots are vital for preserving the continent's exceptional biodiversity. These efforts not only protect unique species and ecosystems but also contribute to sustainable development and the well-being of local communities. As we continue to navigate the complex challenges of conservation in these precious regions, international cooperation and support are essential to safeguard Africa's natural heritage for generations to come.

CHAPTER 9: THE AMERICAS: A BIODIVERSITY KALEIDOSCOPE

NORTH AMERICAN HOTSPOTS

North America, known for its vast landscapes and rich biodiversity, is home to several remarkable biodiversity hotspots. These regions are characterized by high levels of species diversity and endemism, making them essential areas for conservation efforts. In this exploration, we delve into the North American hotspots and the initiatives aimed at preserving their unique natural heritage.

1. The Significance of North American Hotspots:

Biodiversity hotspots are critical to global conservation efforts for several reasons:

Unique Species: These areas often contain species found nowhere else on Earth, making them invaluable for preserving genetic diversity.

Ecosystem Services: Hotspots provide vital ecosystem services, including clean water, pollination, and climate regulation, benefiting both nature and people.

Research Opportunities: Hotspots offer opportunities for scientific research and discovery, helping us better understand the intricacies of biodiversity.

2. Key North American Biodiversity Hotspots:

North America is home to several notable hotspots, each with its own distinct ecosystems and species:

California Floristic Province: This hotspot, located in California and parts of Oregon and Baja California, is renowned for its diverse plant life, including numerous endemic species. It includes iconic habitats like chaparral and coastal sage scrub.

Madrean Sky Islands: Spanning parts of the southwestern United States and northwestern Mexico, this hotspot consists of isolated mountain ranges (sky islands) surrounded by desert. It's home to a rich variety of flora and fauna adapted to these unique environments.

Florida's Caribbean Islands: This hotspot includes the Florida Keys and the nearby Caribbean islands. It boasts diverse marine life, coral reefs, and endemic species, making it a global conservation priority.

Central Appalachians: This hotspot extends from Pennsylvania to Georgia, encompassing the Appalachian Mountains. It's known for its rich biodiversity, especially among amphibians and salamanders.

3. Conservation Initiatives:

Efforts to protect North American hotspots encompass various strategies:

Protected Areas: Establishing and managing national parks, wildlife refuges, and reserves helps safeguard critical habitats.

Habitat Restoration: Restoration projects aim to revive degraded habitats, allowing native species to recover.

Conservation Partnerships: Collaborative efforts among governments, NGOs, and local communities are crucial for effective conservation.

Climate Resilience: Addressing climate change impacts is essential, as rising temperatures and altered precipitation patterns affect these hotspots.

4. Success Stories:

Conservation initiatives in North American hotspots have yielded positive outcomes:

California Condor Recovery: The California condor, one of the world's most endangered birds, has seen a remarkable recovery thanks to captive breeding and reintroduction efforts.

Red Wolf Conservation: In North Carolina, efforts to reintroduce and protect red wolves have helped stabilize this critically endangered species.

Florida Panther Recovery: Collaborative actions have increased the population of the Florida panther, a subspecies of cougar, in South Florida.

5. Ongoing Challenges:

Despite successes, North American hotspots face persistent challenges:

Habitat Fragmentation: Urbanization and infrastructure development continue to fragment and degrade natural habitats.

Invasive Species: Non-native species can outcompete or prey upon native species, disrupting ecosystems.

Climate Change: Warming temperatures and altered precipitation patterns pose threats to species and habitats.

North American hotspots are vital components of global biodiversity conservation efforts. They showcase the incredible diversity of life on the continent and the importance of preserving these unique ecosystems. As we navigate the ongoing challenges of conservation, it's crucial to prioritize the protection of these hotspots, ensuring that North America's natural heritage remains intact for future generations.

CENTRAL AND SOUTH AMERICAN HOTSPOTS

Central and South America are regions of astounding natural beauty and incredible biodiversity. Within these continents lie several biodiversity hotspots, areas celebrated for their exceptional species richness and unique ecosystems. In this exploration, we delve into Central and South American hotspots, their significance in the world of biodiversity, and the ongoing conservation efforts to protect these invaluable natural treasures.

1. The Significance of Central and South American Hotspots:

Biodiversity hotspots are crucial for global biodiversity conservation for various reasons:

Unique Species: These regions often harbor species found nowhere else on Earth, making them vital for preserving genetic diversity.

Ecosystem Services: Hotspots provide essential ecosystem services, including carbon sequestration, water purification, and climate regulation, benefiting both nature and human society.

Cultural Heritage: Many of these hotspots are home to indigenous communities with deep cultural connections to their environments, highlighting the profound relationship between people and nature.

2. Key Central and South American Biodiversity Hotspots:

Central and South America boast several renowned biodiversity hotspots, each with its own distinctive ecosystems:

Amazon Rainforest: The Amazon is the world's largest tropical rainforest, stretching across nine countries. It is renowned for its staggering diversity of flora, fauna, and indigenous cultures.

Mesoamerica: Spanning from southern Mexico through Central America, this hotspot is characterized by rich biodiversity and ancient Mayan ruins.

Chocó-Darién-Western Ecuador: Extending along the Pacific coast from Panama to Ecuador, this hotspot is known for its lush rainforests and high levels of endemism, especially among amphibians.

Atlantic Forest: Covering portions of Brazil, Paraguay, and Argentina, the Atlantic Forest is a global biodiversity hotspot with numerous endemic species.

3. Conservation Initiatives:

Preserving Central and South American hotspots necessitates a comprehensive approach to conservation:

Protected Areas: Establishing and effectively managing national parks, reserves, and wildlife corridors is essential to safeguard critical habitats.

Forest Restoration: Efforts to restore degraded forests can enhance habitat quality and reconnect fragmented landscapes.

Community-Based Conservation: Collaborative efforts involving local communities promote sustainable land use, empower indigenous knowledge, and foster conservation partnerships.

Scientific Research: Ongoing research is crucial for monitoring biodiversity, comprehending ecosystem dynamics, and guiding conservation strategies.

4. Success Stories:

Conservation initiatives in Central and South American hotspots have yielded significant achievements:

Araucaria Forest Protection: Conservation endeavors have helped safeguard the unique Araucaria forests in southern Brazil, preserving the endangered Brazilian pine.

Yaguas National Park: In Peru, the establishment of Yaguas National Park protects a vast expanse of Amazon rainforest, conserving biodiversity and indigenous territories.

Indigenous-Led Conservation: Indigenous communities across Central and South America play pivotal roles in conservation, bridging traditional knowledge with modern science.

5. Ongoing Challenges:

Despite progress, Central and South American hotspots confront enduring conservation challenges:

Deforestation: Logging, agriculture, and infrastructure development continue to pose threats to natural habitats.

Illegal Wildlife Trade: Poaching and the illegal trade of wildlife and their parts remain significant threats to numerous species.

Climate Change: Shifting climate patterns, rising temperatures, and altered precipitation regimes affect species distribution and ecosystem resilience.

Central and South American hotspots represent ecological jewels, brimming with distinctive species and vibrant cultures. Conservation endeavors in these regions are not only pivotal for preserving biodiversity but also for safeguarding the well-being of local communities and the ecological stability of our planet.

As we navigate the intricate conservation challenges, international collaboration and support are indispensable to ensure that these hotspots continue to flourish for generations to come.

CONSERVATION ACROSS THE AMERICAS

The Americas, comprising North, Central, and South America, encompass a vast and diverse landscape of ecosystems and wildlife. To safeguard the incredible biodiversity and ecological treasures of this vast continent, conservation efforts have transcended borders. In this exploration, we delve into the collaborative initiatives and shared challenges of conservation across the Americas.

1. The Uniting Force of Biodiversity:

The Americas are home to some of the world's most significant biodiversity hotspots, including the Amazon rainforest, Central American cloud forests, and the Chocó-Darién-Western Ecuador region. The unique species and ecosystems of this continent have drawn global attention, emphasizing the need for coordinated conservation efforts.

2. Shared Conservation Challenges:

Conservation challenges in the Americas often transcend political boundaries:

Habitat Loss: Deforestation, urbanization, and agricultural expansion threaten natural habitats and ecosystems, impacting both flora and fauna.

Climate Change: Rising temperatures, changing precipitation patterns, and extreme weather events affect ecosystems and species distribution.

Illegal Wildlife Trade: Poaching and the illegal trade of wildlife and their parts pose threats to numerous species, including iconic ones like jaguars, condors, and sea turtles.

Invasive Species: Non-native species can disrupt ecosystems, outcompete native species, and alter natural habitats.

3. Collaborative Initiatives:

Conservation organizations, governments, and local communities across the Americas have come together to address these shared challenges:

Transboundary Conservation Areas: The establishment of protected areas and reserves that span multiple countries promotes the conservation of migratory species and biodiversity.

International Agreements: Multilateral agreements and conventions, such as the Convention on International Trade in Endangered Species of Wild Fauna and Flora (CITES), facilitate cooperation in wildlife conservation.

Community Involvement: Engaging local communities in conservation efforts fosters stewardship and sustainable land use practices.

Scientific Collaboration: Researchers from different countries collaborate on studies and initiatives, contributing to a better understanding of biodiversity and ecosystem dynamics.

4. Success Stories:

Collaborative conservation efforts in the Americas have yielded remarkable successes:

Manuel Antonio National Park (Costa Rica): Transboundary conservation with Panama has led to the protection of critical habitats for various species, including the endangered squirrel monkey.

The Path of the Pronghorn (USA and Mexico): This transboundary corridor connects pronghorn populations across the U.S.-Mexico border, aiding their migration and genetic diversity.

Mesoamerican Biological Corridor (Central America): This initiative aims to connect protected areas and promote biodiversity conservation through international cooperation.

5. Ongoing Challenges:

While progress has been made, conservation in the Americas continues to face challenges:

Resource Limitations: Many conservation initiatives require substantial funding and resources, which can be limited in some regions.

Policy Coordination: Aligning environmental policies and regulations across borders can be complex and require ongoing diplomacy.

Human-Wildlife Conflict: In some areas, the coexistence of people and wildlife can lead to conflicts, especially when agriculture and livelihoods are impacted.

Conservation across the Americas reflects the recognition that the protection of biodiversity knows no borders. Collaborative efforts are essential to addressing shared conservation challenges, preserving the rich natural heritage of this continent, and ensuring a sustainable future for the diverse ecosystems and species that call the Americas home.

By working together, the countries of the Americas demonstrate their commitment to the conservation of our planet's most precious treasures.

CHAPTER 10: ASIA: THE CRADLE OF BIODIVERSITY

THE HIMALAYAS AND SOUTHEAST ASIA

The Himalayas and Southeast Asia are two interconnected regions renowned for their breathtaking landscapes, rich biodiversity, and diverse cultures. Stretching from the lofty peaks of the Himalayas to the tropical rainforests of Southeast Asia, this vast expanse of terrain hosts a tapestry of natural wonders and human traditions. In this exploration, we dive into the uniqueness and significance of the Himalayas and Southeast Asia.

1. The Majesty of the Himalayas:

The Himalayan Mountain range, often referred to as the "abode of snow," is the world's highest and most iconic mountain range. Key features and aspects include:

Geological Marvel: The Himalayas were formed by the collision of the Indian and Eurasian tectonic plates, resulting in some of the world's tallest peaks, including Mount Everest.

Biodiversity Haven: Despite the harsh conditions, the Himalayas are a hotspot of biodiversity with a wide range of flora and fauna adapted to high altitudes.

Cultural Diversity: The Himalayas are home to diverse ethnic groups, each with its own languages, traditions, and spiritual practices. Tibetan Buddhism, Hinduism, and other belief systems flourish here.

2. The Splendor of Southeast Asia:

Southeast Asia, situated south of China and east of India, is a region of extraordinary biodiversity and cultural diversity. Key features and aspects include:

Tropical Rainforests: Southeast Asia boasts some of the world's most extensive tropical rainforests, home to a staggering array of plant and animal species.

Cultural Melting Pot: The region's history is marked by the confluence of various cultures, including Indian, Chinese, Indonesian, and indigenous traditions.

Maritime Heritage: Southeast Asia has a rich maritime heritage, with its people relying on waterways for trade, transportation, and sustenance.

3. Shared Biodiversity:

The Himalayas and Southeast Asia share a remarkable overlap of biodiversity, despite the geographic distance between them. This phenomenon is known as the "Himalayan-Southeast Asian Biodiversity Hotspot" and is characterized by unique species and ecosystems that span both regions.

4. Conservation Challenges:

Both the Himalayas and Southeast Asia face a range of conservation challenges:

Habitat Loss: Deforestation, urbanization, and agriculture continue to threaten natural habitats in both regions.

Climate Change: Rising temperatures and altered precipitation patterns impact glaciers in the Himalayas and the stability of ecosystems in Southeast Asia.

Illegal Wildlife Trade: Poaching and the illegal trade of wildlife and their parts remain significant threats to numerous species, including tigers, rhinoceroses, and pangolins.

5. Conservation Efforts:

Conservation initiatives in the Himalayas and Southeast Asia aim to address these shared challenges:

Protected Areas: Establishing and managing national parks, wildlife reserves, and marine sanctuaries help protect critical habitats.

Community Engagement: Involving local communities in conservation efforts promotes sustainable land use and fosters stewardship.

Scientific Research: Ongoing research helps monitor biodiversity, understand ecosystem dynamics, and guide conservation strategies.

6. Cultural Significance:

Both regions hold immense cultural significance:

Spirituality: The Himalayas are considered sacred in various religions and spiritual traditions, drawing pilgrims and seekers from around the world.

Traditional Wisdom: Indigenous communities in Southeast Asia possess a wealth of traditional knowledge about plants, animals, and ecosystems, contributing to conservation efforts.

The Himalayas and Southeast Asia are jewels of natural beauty, biodiversity, and cultural heritage. Their interconnectedness through the Himalayan-Southeast Asian Biodiversity Hotspot underscores the importance of collaborative conservation efforts. As we navigate the complex challenges of preserving these regions, it is essential to prioritize the protection of their unique ecosystems and cultures for the well-being of both people and nature.

THE SUNDALAND BIODIVERSITY HOTSPOT

The Sundaland Biodiversity Hotspot is a region of extraordinary biological diversity that encompasses parts of Southeast Asia. Named after the ancient Sundaland landmass, which once connected the Indonesian archipelago to the Asian mainland, this hotspot is celebrated for its rich tapestry of unique species and ecosystems. In this exploration, we delve into the Sundaland Biodiversity Hotspot, its significance, and the conservation challenges it faces.

1. Location and Geography:

The Sundaland Hotspot stretches across the islands of Borneo, Sumatra, Java, and the Malay Peninsula, as well as parts of Thailand, Cambodia, and Vietnam. Its diverse landscapes include tropical rainforests, wetlands, mangroves, and limestone karsts.

2. Biodiversity Riches:

The Sundaland Hotspot is renowned for its extraordinary biodiversity:

Flora: It hosts an immense variety of plant species, including countless orchids, pitcher plants, and dipterocarps (tropical hardwood trees).

Fauna: The region is home to iconic and endangered species such as orangutans, tigers, Sumatran rhinoceroses, and proboscis monkeys. It is also a hotspot for bird diversity, with species like the helmeted hornbill and the Javan hawk-eagle.

Freshwater Biodiversity: The Sundaland Hotspot's rivers and wetlands are teeming with unique fish species, including numerous colorful and endemic freshwater fish.

Marine Life: The coastal and marine areas of the hotspot are equally rich, featuring vibrant coral reefs and a plethora of marine species, including seahorses, mantis shrimp, and dugongs

3. Significance:

The Sundaland Biodiversity Hotspot is of global importance for several reasons:

Endemism: It boasts a high degree of endemism, with many species found nowhere else on Earth. These unique species contribute to the hotspot's distinctiveness.

Ecosystem Services: The forests and wetlands of Sundaland provide vital ecosystem services, including carbon sequestration, water purification, and climate regulation, benefiting both the region and the planet.

4. Conservation Challenges:

Despite its importance, the Sundaland Hotspot faces numerous conservation challenges:

Habitat Loss: Deforestation, agriculture, logging, and infrastructure development continue to threaten natural habitats.

Illegal Wildlife Trade: Poaching and the illegal trade of wildlife and their parts pose significant threats to iconic species like tigers and rhinoceroses.

Climate Change: Rising temperatures and altered precipitation patterns impact the region's ecosystems and species.

5. Conservation Efforts:

Conservation initiatives in the Sundaland Biodiversity Hotspot aim to address these challenges:

Protected Areas: Establishing and effectively managing national parks, wildlife reserves, and marine sanctuaries help protect critical habitats.

Community-Based Conservation: Involving local communities in conservation efforts promotes sustainable land use and fosters stewardship.

Scientific Research: Ongoing research helps monitor biodiversity, understand ecosystem dynamics, and guide conservation strategies.

6. Success Stories:

Despite challenges, there have been successes in the conservation of the Sundaland Hotspot:

Orangutan Conservation: Efforts to protect orangutan habitats and combat illegal wildlife trade have contributed to the stabilization of orangutan populations.

Tiger Conservation: Anti-poaching and habitat protection measures have helped maintain tiger populations in some areas.

The Sundaland Biodiversity Hotspot is a tropical paradise of unique life and natural wonders. Preserving this remarkable region is not only essential for the survival of countless species but also for maintaining the ecological balance of our planet. Collaborative conservation efforts, international support, and the engagement of local communities are crucial to ensuring that the Sundaland Hotspot remains a thriving and biodiverse haven for generations to come.

ASIAN CONSERVATION SUCCESS STORIES

Asia, the world's largest and most diverse continent, is home to a wealth of unique species and ecosystems. Despite facing numerous conservation challenges, there have been remarkable success stories in the region. In this exploration, we celebrate Asian conservation successes that demonstrate the power of dedicated efforts in protecting biodiversity.

1. The Return of the Giant Panda (China):

Perhaps one of the most iconic symbols of conservation success, the giant panda has made a remarkable recovery in China. Key achievements include:

Habitat Restoration: Efforts to protect and restore bamboo forests, the panda's primary habitat, have expanded protected areas.

Breeding Programs: Captive breeding and reintroduction programs have increased the panda population, reducing its endangered status.

Public Awareness: The panda's global recognition has raised awareness and support for conservation initiatives.

2. Tigers Making a Comeback (India and Nepal):

Tiger populations have rebounded in some Asian countries, particularly in India and Nepal:

Anti-Poaching Measures: Enhanced law enforcement, patrolling, and community involvement have reduced tiger poaching.

Habitat Protection: The creation of protected tiger reserves and corridors has expanded their habitats.

Technological Innovations: The use of camera traps and DNA analysis has improved monitoring and conservation efforts.

3. Saola Rediscovered (Laos and Vietnam):

The saola, an enigmatic and critically endangered antelope-like species, was rediscovered in the Annamite Mountains, a region straddling Laos and Vietnam.

Community Engagement: Local communities have been engaged in conservation efforts, helping protect saola habitat and report sightings.

Research and Monitoring: Conservationists have employed camera traps and surveys to gather critical data on saola populations.

4. Amur Leopard Recovery (Russia and China):

The Amur leopard, one of the world's most endangered big cats, has experienced a slight increase in numbers:

Cross-Border Collaboration: Russia and China have worked together to strengthen law enforcement and habitat protection.

Camera Traps: The use of camera traps has been instrumental in monitoring the elusive Amur leopards.

5. Successful Marine Conservation (Various Asian Countries):

Several Asian countries have made strides in marine conservation:

Coral Reef Protection: Indonesia, the Philippines, and Malaysia have established marine protected areas and implemented sustainable fishing practices to protect coral reefs.

Marine Sanctuaries: Countries like Thailand and the Maldives have created marine sanctuaries to safeguard marine life.

Sea Turtle Conservation: Efforts to protect sea turtles and their nesting sites in countries like Sri Lanka and Oman have yielded positive results.

6. Sustainable Forestry in Bhutan:

Bhutan has embraced sustainable forestry practices, maintaining a forest cover of over 70%:

Community-Based Management: Local communities play a key role in forest management, benefiting from sustainable timber harvesting and eco-tourism.

Carbon Neutrality: Bhutan's commitment to carbon neutrality has further incentivized sustainable forest management.

7. Asian Elephant Conservation in Thailand:

Thailand has implemented various measures to protect its Asian elephant populations:

Elephant Sanctuaries: Elephant sanctuaries have been established to provide rescued elephants with a safe and natural environment.

Tourism Regulation: Regulations have been enacted to ensure that elephant tourism activities are humane and sustainable.

These Asian conservation success stories demonstrate the power of dedication, collaboration, and innovation in protecting the region's unique biodiversity. While challenges persist, these achievements inspire hope and serve as models for future conservation efforts. By continuing to work together, Asia can further strengthen its commitment to biodiversity protection and ensure a sustainable future for its incredible natural heritage.

CHAPTER 11: OCEANIA: PACIFIC PARADISES

ISLAND NATIONS AND THEIR UNIQUE BIODIVERSITY

Island nations scattered across the world's oceans are known for their exceptional biodiversity and distinct ecosystems. These isolated landmasses have nurtured unique flora and fauna, often found nowhere else on Earth. In this exploration, we delve into the biodiversity of island nations, the challenges they face, and the importance of their conservation.

1. Island Nations and Their Biodiversity:

Island nations, whether in the Pacific, Indian, Atlantic, or other oceans, have evolved unique ecosystems due to their isolation:

Endemic Species: Many island nations are home to species found nowhere else, known as endemics. These species have adapted to their isolated environments over millions of years.

Diverse Marine Life: Coral reefs, coastal habitats, and surrounding waters teem with diverse marine life, including colorful fish, turtles, and whales.

Distinct Flora: Islands often have their own unique plant species, from tropical rainforest flora to arid desert succulents.

2. Challenges to Island Biodiversity:

Island nations face several conservation challenges:

Habitat Loss: Urbanization, agriculture, and infrastructure development encroach on natural habitats.

Invasive Species: Non-native species introduced by humans can outcompete native flora and fauna, leading to ecosystem disruption.

Climate Change: Rising sea levels and altered weather patterns threaten coastal ecosystems and wildlife.

3. Pacific Islands:

Hawaii: Known for its diverse range of species, Hawaii's unique ecosystems include the silversword plant and the Hawaiian monk seal.

Fiji: The Fiji archipelago harbors a wealth of marine life, including colorful coral reefs, reef sharks, and sea turtles.

4. Indian Ocean Islands:

Madagascar: Often called the "eighth continent," Madagascar boasts unique lemurs, chameleons, and baobab trees.

Seychelles: These islands are a haven for marine biodiversity, with coral reefs, rare tortoises, and unique bird species.

5. Atlantic Islands:

Galápagos Islands (Ecuador): Made famous by Charles Darwin, the Galápagos are a living laboratory of evolution, with species like giant tortoises, marine iguanas, and blue-footed boobies.

Azores (Portugal): These islands in the North Atlantic are known for their lush landscapes, endemic flora, and migratory marine life.

6. Conservation Efforts:

Efforts to protect island biodiversity include:

Protected Areas: Establishing marine and terrestrial reserves helps safeguard critical habitats.

Invasive Species Management: Programs to control and eradicate invasive species are crucial for ecosystem restoration.

Community Involvement: Engaging local communities in conservation fosters stewardship and sustainable practices.

Climate Adaptation: Developing strategies to mitigate the impact of climate change on coastal areas and marine ecosystems.

7. Tourism and Conservation:

Sustainable tourism can provide economic benefits while preserving fragile island ecosystems. Regulations and responsible tourism practices are essential to strike a balance.

Island nations are ecological treasures that showcase the wonders of evolution and adaptation.

Protecting their unique biodiversity is not only essential for the sake of science but also for the well-being of local communities and the health of our planet. By recognizing the value of these fragile ecosystems and committing to their conservation, we can ensure that the rich natural heritage of island nations endures for future generations to appreciate and cherish.

THE PACIFIC HOTSPOT CHALLENGE

The Pacific Ocean, with its idyllic islands and azure waters, is not only a paradise for beachgoers but also a hotspot of biodiversity. The Pacific Hotspot, also known as the "Polynesia-Micronesia Hotspot," encompasses numerous islands scattered across the vast expanse of the Pacific Ocean. These islands are home to a remarkable array of unique species and ecosystems. However, they also face formidable conservation challenges. In this exploration, we delve into the Pacific Hotspot Challenge, its significance, and ongoing efforts to protect this ecological treasure.

1. The Pacific Hotspot: A Biodiversity Paradise:

The Pacific Hotspot spans a vast region, including islands such as Hawaii, Fiji, Samoa, the Solomon Islands, and many more. This region is characterized by its exceptional biodiversity, featuring:

Endemic Species: Many species found in the Pacific Hotspot are endemic, meaning they are found nowhere else on Earth. This high level of endemism is due to the isolation of these islands.

Marine Riches: Coral reefs, clear lagoons, and rich marine life, including vibrant fish, sharks, and turtles, are hallmarks of this hotspot.

Unique Flora: Island nations in the Pacific are known for their distinct plant species, from tropical rainforest trees to desert-adapted succulents.

2. Conservation Challenges in Paradise:

Despite its natural beauty, the Pacific Hotspot faces several pressing conservation challenges:

Habitat Loss: As populations grow, urbanization, agriculture, and infrastructure development encroach on natural habitats.

Invasive Species: Non-native species introduced by humans can disrupt fragile island ecosystems, outcompeting native flora and fauna.

Climate Change: Rising sea levels, ocean acidification, and extreme weather events pose threats to coastal ecosystems and wildlife.

3. Conservation Initiatives:

Efforts to protect the biodiversity of the Pacific Hotspot include:

Protected Areas: Establishing marine and terrestrial reserves, such as national parks and marine sanctuaries, helps preserve critical habitats.

Invasive Species Management: Programs to control and eradicate invasive species are essential for ecosystem restoration.

Community Engagement: Involving local communities in conservation fosters stewardship and sustainable practices.

Scientific Research: Ongoing research helps monitor biodiversity, understand ecosystem dynamics, and guide conservation strategies.

4. Success Stories:

There have been notable successes in conserving the Pacific Hotspot:

Papahānaumokuākea Marine National Monument (Hawaii): This vast marine protected area safeguards critical habitats and is home to unique marine species.

Palmyra Atoll (U.S. Minor Outlying Islands): Efforts to eradicate invasive rats have allowed native vegetation and bird populations to rebound.

5. Challenges for Island Nations:

Pacific island nations, which are highly vulnerable to climate change and rising sea levels, face additional challenges:

Cultural Heritage: Many island nations have rich indigenous cultures deeply connected to their natural surroundings. Protecting biodiversity is intertwined with preserving cultural heritage.

Sustainable Development: Balancing economic development with conservation is a complex challenge, especially for small island nations.

The Pacific Hotspot Challenge underscores the importance of protecting biodiversity in this paradise of islands. It is not only crucial for the survival of unique species but also for the well-being of local communities and the ecological health of our planet. By recognizing the significance of these fragile ecosystems and committing to their conservation, we can ensure that the Pacific Hotspot continues to thrive as a haven of biodiversity and natural wonder for generations to come.

INDIGENOUS KNOWLEDGE AND CONSERVATION IN OCEANIA

Oceania, a vast region of islands and atolls scattered across the Pacific Ocean, is home to a rich tapestry of indigenous cultures. These diverse communities have inhabited these islands for millennia, developing a profound understanding of their natural environments. Indigenous knowledge, passed down through generations, plays a crucial role in the conservation of Oceania's unique biodiversity. In this exploration, we delve into the relationship between indigenous knowledge and conservation in the Pacific Islands.

1. Indigenous Cultures of Oceania:

Oceania is home to an incredible diversity of indigenous cultures, including the Maori of New Zealand, the Polynesians of Hawaii, the Samoans, the Fijians, and many more. These cultures have deeply rooted connections to their land and seas.

2. Indigenous Knowledge and Conservation:

Indigenous communities in Oceania possess a wealth of traditional knowledge about their natural surroundings, which includes:

Species Identification: Indigenous peoples have in-depth knowledge of local flora and fauna, including medicinal plants and edible species.

Traditional Ecological Practices: Time-tested agricultural and land management practices that promote sustainability and prevent soil erosion.

Navigational Skills: Traditional wayfinding techniques, such as star mapping and wave patterns, have allowed Pacific Islanders to navigate vast oceans without modern instruments.

Cultural Practices: Many indigenous cultures have sacred sites and rituals that protect certain areas from exploitation, acting as de facto conservation measures.

3. Sustainable Resource Management:

Indigenous communities in Oceania have long been practicing sustainable resource management:

Fishing Practices: Sustainable fishing practices, such as seasonal bans and size limits, are common among Pacific Island communities.

Agriculture: Crop rotation, traditional seed saving, and agroforestry techniques help maintain soil fertility and crop diversity.

4. Modern Conservation Partnerships:

In recent years, there has been a growing recognition of the value of indigenous knowledge in conservation efforts:

Collaborative Conservation: Many conservation organizations are working hand in hand with indigenous communities to develop and implement conservation plans.

Protected Areas: Indigenous-managed protected areas are increasingly recognized and supported for their effectiveness in preserving biodiversity.

5. Challenges and Threats:

Despite their profound knowledge and conservation efforts, indigenous communities in Oceania face several challenges:

Climate Change: Rising sea levels and changing weather patterns threaten the very existence of low-lying island nations.

Invasive Species: The introduction of non-native species poses a threat to native flora and fauna.

Economic Pressures: Globalization and economic pressures can sometimes lead to unsustainable resource exploitation.

6. Cultural Resilience:

Despite these challenges, many indigenous communities in Oceania are demonstrating cultural resilience:

Cultural Revival: Efforts to preserve and revive traditional practices, languages, and rituals are on the rise.

Environmental Stewardship: Indigenous communities are increasingly recognized as guardians of their lands and seas, with an integral role in conservation efforts.

Indigenous knowledge is a precious asset in the conservation of Oceania's biodiversity. The wisdom of these communities, honed over generations, offers valuable insights into sustainable living and environmental protection. Recognizing the importance of indigenous knowledge and fostering collaborative conservation efforts with these communities is essential to preserve the natural beauty and ecological richness of the Pacific Islands for future generations.

CHAPTER 12: THE FUTURE OF BIODIVERSITY HOTSPOTS

THREATS AND CHALLENGES AHEAD

As we look to the future of conservation, it becomes increasingly evident that the natural world faces a multitude of threats and challenges. These issues are complex, interconnected, and require concerted efforts from individuals, communities, governments, and the global community. In this exploration, we delve into the pressing threats and challenges that lie ahead for conservation.

1. Habitat Loss and Fragmentation:

Deforestation: The relentless clearing of forests for agriculture, urban development, and logging continues to fragment and destroy vital habitats for countless species.

Urbanization: As urban populations grow, cities expand, consuming valuable land and natural habitats.

2. Climate Change:

Rising Temperatures: Global warming disrupts ecosystems, changes migration patterns, and poses threats to species ill-equipped to adapt.

Sea-Level Rise: Coastal habitats are threatened as sea levels rise, endangering both terrestrial and marine species.

3. Pollution and Habitat Degradation:

Pollution: Water and air pollution harm aquatic and terrestrial ecosystems, impacting the health of species and ecosystems.

Habitat Degradation: Land degradation, soil erosion, and overfertilization degrade habitats and reduce their capacity to support biodiversity.

4. Invasive Species:

Non-native species introduced by humans can outcompete native species, disrupt ecosystems, and lead to the decline or extinction of indigenous flora and fauna.

5. Overexploitation:

Overfishing: Unsustainable fishing practices threaten marine ecosystems and the livelihoods of coastal communities.

Illegal Wildlife Trade: Poaching and illegal trade in wildlife and their parts remain major threats to numerous species, from elephants and rhinoceroses to pangolins and parrots.

6. Cultural and Societal Factors:

Disconnect from Nature: An increasing detachment from the natural world in urbanized societies can lead to a lack of appreciation and understanding of the importance of biodiversity.

Population Growth: The growth of the human population places additional stress on natural resources and habitats.

7. Economic and Political Pressures:

Short-Term Focus: Economic and political systems often prioritize short-term gains over long-term environmental sustainability.

Global Inequities: The unequal distribution of resources and access to conservation efforts can hinder progress.

8. Emerging Diseases and Pandemics:

The spillover of diseases from wildlife to humans, as seen with zoonotic diseases like COVID-19, underscores the interconnectedness of human and ecological health.

9. Technological Advancements:

While technology can aid conservation efforts, it can also pose new challenges, such as the use of drones for illegal activities like poaching.

10. Changing Conservation Landscape:

The conservation community must adapt to evolving challenges, engage with new stakeholders, and embrace innovative approaches to achieve its goals.

11. Hope for the Future:

Community-Led Conservation: Empowering local communities to take ownership of conservation efforts is crucial.

Science and Technology: Advances in monitoring, data analysis, and conservation techniques offer new opportunities.

Policy and Advocacy: Lobbying for stronger environmental regulations and policies is essential.

Public Awareness: Education and awareness campaigns can foster a deeper appreciation for the natural world.

Conservation faces a multitude of threats and challenges, but there is hope in collective action, innovation, and a shared commitment to preserving the planet's biodiversity. By recognizing these challenges and working collaboratively across borders and sectors, we can strive for a more sustainable and harmonious relationship with the natural world, ensuring that future generations inherit a planet rich in biological diversity and ecological health.

Conservation Strategies and Hopeful Solutions

In the face of mounting environmental challenges, conservationists and communities worldwide are developing innovative strategies and solutions to protect and restore our planet's precious biodiversity. While the threats are real and daunting, there is hope in the form of proactive measures and collaborative efforts. In this exploration, we delve into some of the conservation strategies and hopeful solutions that offer promise for a sustainable future.

1. Protected Areas and Habitat Restoration:

Expanding Protected Areas: Establishing and maintaining protected areas, such as national parks and marine reserves, helps safeguard critical habitats.

Habitat Restoration: Efforts to restore degraded ecosystems, including reforestation and wetland restoration, can revitalize habitats and support biodiversity.

2. Sustainable Land Use:

Agroforestry and Sustainable Farming: Integrating trees and diverse crops can enhance agricultural sustainability and preserve biodiversity.

Eco-Friendly Urban Planning: Creating green spaces within cities and adopting sustainable urban development practices can mitigate habitat loss.

3. Community Engagement:

Local Stewardship: Empowering local communities to actively manage and protect their natural resources fosters a sense of ownership and sustainability.

Indigenous Knowledge: Recognizing and respecting the traditional ecological knowledge of indigenous communities can inform conservation efforts.

4. Combating Climate Change:

Renewable Energy: Transitioning to renewable energy sources reduces carbon emissions and mitigates climate change impacts on ecosystems.

Climate-Resilient Conservation: Implementing conservation strategies that account for climate change, such as assisted migration for species under threat, is crucial.

5. Technology and Innovation:

AI and Machine Learning: Advanced technology aids in wildlife monitoring, anti-poaching efforts, and data analysis for more effective conservation.

Genomic Conservation: Utilizing genetic techniques can help preserve endangered species and restore genetic diversity.

6. Policy and Advocacy:

Stronger Regulations: Advocating for stronger environmental laws and regulations at local, national, and international levels is essential.

Economic Incentives: Promoting sustainable practices through economic incentives and penalties encourages responsible resource management.

7. Public Awareness and Education:

Environmental Education: Educating the public, especially the younger generation, about the importance of biodiversity and conservation fosters a culture of stewardship.

Communication and Outreach: Conservation organizations and scientists increasingly use storytelling and multimedia to engage a broader audience.

8. Global Collaboration:

International Agreements: Multilateral agreements, such as the Convention on Biological Diversity and the Paris Agreement, foster global cooperation in conservation and climate action.

Transboundary Conservation: Collaborative conservation efforts that span borders help protect migratory species and ecosystems.

9. Hopeful Success Stories:

The Recovery of the California Condor: A once-critically endangered species, the California condor, has made a remarkable recovery through captive breeding and reintroduction efforts.

The Growth of Marine Protected Areas: Countries around the world are expanding their marine protected areas to safeguard ocean ecosystems.

10. The Role of Youth:

Young activists and conservationists are playing an increasingly prominent role in advocating for change and driving conservation efforts forward.

While conservation faces significant challenges, the combination of innovative strategies, collaborative initiatives, and growing public awareness offers hope for the preservation of our planet's biodiversity.

It is a collective responsibility to take action and embrace sustainable practices in our daily lives. Through global cooperation, policy reform, technological advances, and a shared commitment to the well-being of the natural world, we can work toward a future where people and nature coexist harmoniously, ensuring the survival of Earth's diverse ecosystems and the species that call them home.

HOW WE CAN MAKE A DIFFERENCE

In the face of global environmental challenges, it's easy to feel overwhelmed. However, each one of us can play a significant role in conserving biodiversity and mitigating the threats our planet faces. Making a difference begins with individual actions, but it also extends to collective efforts that can drive meaningful change. Here are ways in which we can contribute to conservation:

1. Reduce, Reuse, Recycle:

Waste Reduction: Reduce single-use plastic consumption, opt for reusable products, and properly recycle materials to minimize waste.

2. Sustainable Consumption:

Mindful Shopping: Support products and companies that adhere to sustainable and eco-friendly practices.

3. Energy Conservation:

Energy Efficiency: Reduce energy consumption at home and work by using energy-efficient appliances and practices.

Renewable Energy: Support the use and development of renewable energy sources like solar and wind power.

4. Sustainable Transportation:

Reduce Emissions: opt for public transportation, carpooling, biking, or walking to reduce carbon emissions.

5. Wildlife-Friendly Choices:

Responsible Tourism: Choose wildlife-friendly tourism experiences that prioritize animal welfare and conservation.

Sustainable Seafood: Make informed choices about seafood to support sustainable fisheries and protect marine life.

6. Conservation Advocacy:

Educate Yourself: Stay informed about conservation issues, wildlife, and environmental policies.

Support Conservation Organizations: Contribute to or volunteer with conservation organizations that align with your values and interests.

7. Habitat Restoration:

Local Initiatives: Participate in community-based restoration projects to rejuvenate natural habitats.

8. Sustainable Gardening:

Native Plants: Plant native species in your garden to attract local wildlife and promote biodiversity.

9. Responsible Pet Ownership:

Adoption: Adopt pets from shelters and rescue organizations to reduce demand for breeding.

Spaying and Neutering: Ensure your pets are spayed or neutered to prevent overpopulation.

10. Reduce Water Consumption:

Water Efficiency: Install water-efficient fixtures and be mindful of water use in your daily routines.

11. Education and Outreach:

Engage Others: Share your knowledge about conservation and inspire friends and family to take action.

12. Support Policy Change:

Advocacy: Engage with policymakers and advocate for stronger environmental regulations and conservation policies.

13. Volunteer and Participate:

Community Engagement: Participate in local conservation events, cleanups, and awareness campaigns.

14. Sustainable Agriculture:

Support Local Farmers: Buy locally grown produce to reduce the carbon footprint of your food.

Meat Consumption: Consider reducing meat consumption, as the meat industry has significant environmental impacts.

15. Carbon Offset:

Offset Your Carbon Footprint: Support carbon offset initiatives or tree planting programs to counterbalance your emissions.

16. Eco-Friendly Habits:

Conservation-Minded Choices: Incorporate conservation into your daily life, from turning off lights when not in use to reducing water waste.

17. Education for Future Generations:

Teach Children: Instill a love and respect for nature in children to ensure they become stewards of the environment.

18. Lead by Example:

Inspire Others: Your actions can inspire those around you to make positive changes in their lives.

Individual actions, no matter how small, collectively have the power to make a significant impact on conservation efforts. By adopting sustainable practices, supporting conservation organizations, advocating for change, and inspiring others, we can create a ripple effect of positive change that benefits both the natural world and future generations. Together, we can be catalysts for a more sustainable and biodiverse planet.

CONCLUSION

In "Examining Biodiversity Hotspot: Nature's Distinctiveness Scan," Tom Ferry J has taken us on an illuminating journey through some of the world's most remarkable and fragile ecosystems. From the lush canopies of rainforests to the depths of coral reefs, and from the arid expanses of deserts to the grandeur of mountain landscapes, this book has been a vivid exploration of Earth's biodiversity hotspots.

Throughout these pages, we have witnessed the awe-inspiring richness of life on our planet, marveling at the countless species that call these hotspots home. We have come to understand the importance of these regions as not only reservoirs of unique life but also as critical hubs for maintaining the health of our global environment.

Yet, our exploration hasn't been limited to the wonders of nature alone. We've delved into the complex issues and challenges these hotspots face, from habitat destruction and invasive species to the urgent threat of climate change.

We've examined the extraordinary efforts being made by dedicated individuals, communities, and organizations to protect and preserve these invaluable ecosystems for future generations.

As we close this chapter, it is clear that the fate of biodiversity hotspots is intertwined with the choices we make as a global community. The knowledge and insights presented in this book serve as a call to action. We are reminded that our stewardship of the planet's natural wonders is not an option but an ethical imperative.

Tom Ferry J's work serves as both a tribute to the splendor of biodiversity and a testament to the resilience of those who dedicate their lives to its preservation. It is a call to each of us to embrace our roles as custodians of the Earth and to recognize that, collectively, we have the power to make a profound difference in the conservation of these remarkable hotspots.

May this book inspire us to take action, to support conservation efforts, and to make choices in our own lives that promote the well-being of our planet.

In doing so, we honor the beauty and diversity of life that graces these hotspots and ensure that they continue to thrive, serving as a source of wonder and inspiration for generations to come.